MW00619981

# The Origin of Evil

*By Dr. Chuck Missler*

Koinonia House

**The Origin of Evil**

© Copyright 2017 Koinonia House Inc.

Published by Koinonia House

P.O. Box D

Coeur d'Alene, ID 83816-0347

www.khouse.org

Author: Dr. Chuck Missler

Editor: Amy Joy

ISBN: 978-1-57821-623-9

PRINTED IN THE UNITED STATES OF AMERICA

# Table of Contents

# Chapter 1
# Deliver Us From Evil

Evil is something we understand by nature. We see Sauron or Darth Vader, and we recognize that they are evil. We understand without being told that the bad guys are those who slaughter innocent people. They are the utterly selfish - those whose greed overwhelms them. They prize power and revenge over forgiveness and mercy. We understand this instinctively, even as small children. Nobody thinks that *orcs* are the good guys - not even the orcs.

Of course, evil is not relegated to stories. Real life evil is trickier and hides in better clothes. It might be perpetrated by anybody. People who look pretty, who have good jobs, might be just as likely to do some horrible thing as those with ugly faces and broken cars. We understand that sociopaths are naturally dangerous. But even people who desire to do good, to be kind and loving and generous - even the best of people can do evil things on occasion. We are all capable of cruelty and selfishness, impatience and destruction.

We can scar our consciences so that evil no longer shakes us. We can call evil "good" because it's what we *want* to do. Still, deep inside us, we recognize the difference between right and wrong, good and bad. If we stop to be honest about it, we know.

Why? Why is there evil in this beautiful world? We watch the sunset over the mountains and we wonder about this. How can there be evil in a world where daisies grow wild in meadows? It doesn't fit.

## Satan

We generally avoid the topic of evil. We like telling scary stories around the campfire, but few people enjoy discussions about the reality of wickedness in our world. The subject is fraught with controversy. We can rejoice when Charles Manson is caught, but we don't want to deal with trouble closer to home. We don't want to admit our own rottenness, the foulness in our own hearts. Many people are afraid to talk about the source of evil. They might believe in God, but they don't believe in Satan or Hell.

It's vital that we do talk about evil and its origin. We must never forget that we are in a spiritual battlefield, and knowing how to protect ourselves and our families is so vital that Jesus included it in the prayer He taught His disciples. What did he teach them? "Deliver us from evil."[1] To be more precise, He said, "Deliver us from the evil one."

Who is the evil one?

In *The Far Side*, cartoonist Gary Larson often portrayed Satan as a respectable sort of goblin with horns and a pitchfork, ruling over Hell. That's the media's favorite representation of the Devil, but it's not accurate biblically.

The Bible tells us that Satan is an angel, and Paul tells us in 2 Corinthians 11:14 that Satan can appear as an angel of light. Satan doesn't come to us looking ugly. He's the great deceiver, the father of lies. Jesus describes him succinctly in John 8:44, speaking to the Pharisees:

> *Ye are of your father the devil, and the lusts of your father ye will do. He was a murderer from the beginning, and abode not in the truth, because there is no truth in him. When he speaketh a lie, he speaketh of his own: for he is a liar, and the father of it.*

Satan has many titles. Jesus calls him the "prince of this world" several times in John. [2] Names have great meaning in the Bible, so consider this list of designations given to Satan:

- The god of this world:
  2 Cor 4:4.
- The prince of the power of the air:
  Eph 2:2
- The wicked one:
  Mat 13:19,38; 1 Jhn 2:13-14, 3:12, 5:18
- The enemy:
  Mat 13:39; Luk 10:19
- A murderer:
  Jhn 8:44

- The father of lies:
  Jhn 8:44
- The tempter:
  Mat 4:3
- An adversary like a roaring lion:
  1 Pet 5:8
- The great dragon:
  Rev 12:9
- The serpent:
  Gen 3:1; Rev 12:9, 20:2
- Beelzebub:
  Mat 12:27; Luk 11:18

Satan came to Eve in the garden and convinced her that she couldn't trust God the Creator. Satan doesn't appear to us ugly and scary.[3] Instead, he offers to us everything we think we want. It's only when he's got his claws in us that we realize what a horrible mistake we made in letting him open our window.

Who is Satan? What can he actually do, and what are his limitations? Where did he come from, and most important, how do we protect ourselves from his desire to destroy us? These are the questions this little book seeks to answer.

# Chapter 2
# Evil in our World

As Genesis 3 opens, we find Adam and Eve living in the Garden of Eden, a pristine paradise where God had deemed everything "good." In Genesis 2:20, Adam named all the creatures. God brought each one to him, and we understand from Genesis 9:2-3 that the animals did not fear humans before the Flood. Adam and Eve lived in harmony with the natural world. It was only after the Flood that God gave Noah and his sons the freedom to eat meat - and the fear of man subsequently, where he is called into the instincts of the animals.

Adam and Eve lived in a beautiful garden, and they walked and talked freely with the LORD their Creator. Then came the day the serpent entered their lives:

> *Now the serpent was more subtil than any beast of the field which the LORD God had made. And he said unto the woman, Yea, hath God said, Ye shall not eat of every tree of the garden?*

Genesis 3:1

Here we find Satan at the very beginning of humanity, where he is called merely, "the serpent." We know from Revelation 12:9 and 20:2 that this "old serpent" is indeed Satan, the dragon.

The word for serpent is - נחש - *nachash* - "the shining one." The same root is the basis for the word נחש - *nechash* - "brass." Thus, we find a play on words in Numbers 21:9 when Moses creates a brazen serpent on a pole. He makes נחש *nachash* נחשת *něchosheth* - a serpent of brass. It was called *Nehushtan* by Hezekiah, who had it destroyed in 2 Kings 18:4 because the Israelites had started to worship it.

The same root letters can mean "enchantment" or "enchanter" and so we find the serpent here to beguile Eve. He appears in the Garden and begins speaking with Eve, who is neither frightened by him nor surprised to find an animal talking to her. Eve has no experience with deception or fear or evil. She only knows good company and good food, warm days and cool nights.

The serpent approaches Eve, and the very first thing he does is to draw Eve's attention to the forbidden thing.

He's already setting her up. Of all the trees in the garden, only one had been prohibited to her and Adam. Satan immediately gets Eve to put her attention on this one tree, ignoring the wide array of beautiful trees and delicious fruits freely available to satisfy her:

*And the woman said unto the serpent,*
*We may eat of the fruit of the trees of the*
*garden: But of the fruit of the tree which is*
*in the midst of the garden, God hath said,*
*Ye shall not eat of it, neither shall ye touch*
*it, lest ye die.*

Genesis 3:2-3

In Genesis 2:16-17, God had warned Adam against this single tree. He hadn't mentioned touching the tree's fruit, but He made clear that Adam would die if he ate that particular fruit. Eve was created a few verses later, so we assume she had heard the commandment from the mouth of her husband.

Satan then makes his bold move: he teaches Eve to doubt God's word:

*And the serpent said unto the woman,*
*Ye shall not surely die: For God doth know*
*that in the day ye eat thereof, then your*
*eyes shall be opened, and ye shall be as*
*gods, knowing good and evil.*

Genesis 3:4-5

Here Satan calls into question God's character and works to persuade Eve that God cannot be trusted. First, he calls God a liar by saying, "*Ye shall not surely die.*" Next, he offers an alternate explanation for the commandment: God has been holding out on her and Adam. Satan mixes truth with a lie here, because it *is* true that the tree will give them knowledge of good and evil, but it's not what Eve thinks. Satan insinuates that God doesn't want what is best for them and is keeping her and Adam from greater knowledge. That's the lie Satan tells Eve, and she falls for it.

> *And when the woman saw that the tree*
> *was good for food, and that it was pleasant*
> *to the eyes, and a tree to be desired to make*
> *one wise, she took of the fruit thereof, and*
> *did eat, and gave also unto her husband*
> *with her; and he did eat.*
>
> Genesis 3:6

Eve is deceived. Adam gives in. Both die spiritually that day, and they began to die physically.

If Adam and Eve had been able to look through time and see the rolling avalanche of destruction and suffering caused by that little rock kicked over the mountain, they'd have certainly never touched the fruit of the tree. They would have run and hid their faces in the folds of God's robe. They had no concept of evil - no understanding. They only had knowledge of God's goodness, and they allowed themselves to believe Satan's lie over the righteousness of their Creator.

We are in the same position today. We also choose - every day - whether we will trust God's character. We decide whether we will trust Him to love us, to be faithful to us, to have our best interests in His heart. When things don't go our way and we don't get the things we desire, we can either reject God or we can trust in His goodness. We can forcefully take the things we want, or we can choose to thank Him for His faithful love and wait for His wisdom and guidance.

Genesis 5:5 tells us that Adam lived to be 930 years old. He lived into the lifetime of Lamech, the father of Noah, which means he was able to see some of the long-term consequences of his disobedience. Adam and Eve grieved over the death of their son Abel at the hand of their son Cain, and watched their descendants grow increasingly wicked and violent. It's easy to imagine the anguish in the hearts of Adam and Eve as they saw the once-perfect creation deteriorate. Certainly, a multitude of days passed by in which they wished they had never gained the knowledge of evil.

Of course, there were immediate consequences of their sin. Here in Genesis 3, they suddenly realize that they are naked:

> *And the eyes of them both were opened,*
> *and they knew that they were naked;*
> *and they sewed fig leaves together, and*
> *made themselves aprons. And they heard*
> *the voice of the LORD God walking in*
> *the garden in the cool of the day: and*
> *Adam and his wife hid themselves from*
> *the presence of the LORD God amongst*
> *the trees of the garden. And the LORD*

*God called unto Adam, and said unto
him, Where art thou? And he said, I heard
thy voice in the garden, and I was afraid,
because I was naked; and I hid myself*

Genesis 3:7-10

Adam and Eve have lost their innocence and feel the embarrassment of exposure. They immediately seek to make themselves clothing. Then they hide, because they feel something new. They feel shame.

I suspect that an enormous change took place at the moment Adam and Eve disobeyed God. There are indications that Eden was not simply a location on the planet Earth, but that our first mother and father had access to the additional dimensions that we consider the spiritual realm. After all, they walked with God in the Garden. We learn in Revelation that the Tree of Life still exists in Heaven.[4] We no longer find it here on earth, and mighty cherubim were sent to guard it.[5] It may be Adam and Eve lost access to those additional dimensions, they lost the clothing of the glory that surrounded them, and they realized they were naked. This is just a conjecture on my part, but we do recognize something important; the world we experience today is wholly unlike the one Adam and Eve knew on the Sixth Day of Creation.

*And He said, Who told thee that thou wast
naked? Hast thou eaten of the tree, whereof*

*I commanded thee that thou shouldest not
eat? And the man said, The woman whom
thou gavest to be with me, she gave me of
the tree, and I did eat. And the LORD
God said unto the woman, What is this
that thou hast done? And the woman said,
The serpent beguiled me, and I did eat.*

Genesis 3:11-13

Adam and Eve both know they have done wrong, but their first response is to start pointing fingers. Adam tries to pass the blame to both God and Eve. "*The woman whom thou gavest to be with me-*" Eve, in turn, places blame on the serpent who deceived her.

And so, Satan has succeeded in corrupting the human race from the very beginning.

A variety of verses throughout the Bible confirm our understanding that the serpent is indeed Satan himself. Jesus calls the Devil *"a murderer from the beginning"* and *"the father of liars"* in John 8:44. John clears away any possible confusion in Revelation, clarifying that the dragon is "that old serpent" known as both Satan and the Devil.

*And the great dragon was cast out, that
old serpent, called the Devil, and Satan,
which deceiveth the whole world: he was
cast out into the earth, and his angels were
cast out with him.*

Revelation 12:9

*And he laid hold on the dragon, that old
serpent, which is the Devil, and Satan,
and bound him a thousand years,*

Revelation 20:2

Here in Genesis 3, God gives us the first hint
of Satan's future destruction:

*And the LORD God said unto the serpent,
Because thou hast done this, thou art
cursed above all cattle, and above every
beast of the field; upon thy belly shalt thou
go, and dust shalt thou eat all the days of
thy life: And I will put enmity between
thee and the woman, and between thy seed
and her seed; it shall bruise thy head,
and thou shalt bruise his heel.*

Genesis 3:14-15

This famous prophecy about the seed of the
woman gives us hope for the Messiah even here
at the very beginning of the Bible, immediately
after sin enters the world - and death through sin.
Satan will strike at His heel, but He will crush
Satan's head.[6]

In the meanwhile, life will become much more
difficult for both the woman and her husband:

*Unto the woman he said, I will greatly
multiply thy sorrow and thy conception;
in sorrow thou shalt bring forth children;*

*and thy desire shall be to thy husband,
and he shall rule over thee.*

*And unto Adam he said, Because thou
hast hearkened unto the voice of thy wife,
and hast eaten of the tree, of which I
commanded thee, saying, Thou shalt not
eat of it: cursed is the ground for thy sake;
in sorrow shalt thou eat of it all the days of
thy life;*

*Thorns also and thistles shall it bring forth
to thee; and thou shalt eat the herb of
the field;*

*In the sweat of thy face shalt thou eat
bread, till thou return unto the ground;
for out of it wast thou taken: for dust thou
art, and unto dust shalt thou return.*

*And Adam called his wife's name Eve;
because she was the mother of all living.*

*Unto Adam also and to his wife did
the LORD God make coats of skins,
and clothed them.*

Genesis 3:16-21

They have succeeded in obtaining the
knowledge of good and evil. Congratulations,
they will now have to deal with evil in their new
world. The woman will now face great pain in
her bearing of children. Her relationship with her

husband will change as well; she will want him, but he will rule over her. That wasn't God's original plan. His plan was one of equality: God had made the woman from the rib of Adam as his partner and helpmate. As a result of sin, she will have to face his domination, but she won't want to leave him.

The man is held to the greatest responsibility. God had given Adam the one commandment directly, and he chose to follow his wife's offer over the word of their Creator. He was created to be in harmony with nature; he will now have to battle it to produce his crops. He will have to work hard to make food grow from the ground, fighting thorns and thistles until he dies and returns to the ground from which he was made.

Their new situation has been pronounced; pain, hard work, and death. Yet even here, God demonstrates His own purposes and plans. They attempted to clothe their naked bodies with leaves - which might only last a day or two. God takes the situation in hand and makes clothing for them from skins. Right here at the beginning, God gives us a picture; He will cover our nakedness and our shame, and He will do it through the sacrifice of an innocent.

*And the LORD God said, Behold, the man is become as one of us, to know good and evil: and now, lest he put forth his hand, and take also of the tree of life, and eat, and live for ever: Therefore the LORD God*

*sent him forth from the garden of Eden, to*
*till the ground from whence he was taken.*
*So he drove out the man; and he placed at*
*the east of the garden of Eden Cherubims,*
*and a flaming sword which turned every*
*way, to keep the way of the tree of life.*

Genesis 3:22-24

Eve was curious about the fruit from the forbidden tree. She wanted greater knowledge. She and Adam now both know good and evil, and they can no longer be allowed to access the Tree of Life. They are expelled from the beautiful garden and sent into the world to work for their livelihood.

These things answer the question, "How did evil enter our world?" However, they don't explain the source of the evil itself. Clearly, evil already existed by the time Adam and Eve walked into the picture. It existed in the heart of the serpent who sought to corrupt God's new creation.

# Chapter 3
# Christ's Temptation

Jesus Himself had to deal with the Devil. The crucial difference between us and the Son of God is that He successfully resisted temptation every single time. He has conquered the tempter. He has conquered sin and death. If we are going to successfully combat the enemy's voice in our own ears, we need to pay attention to Jesus and how He handled the difficult situations that came before Him. He is our model in all things.

The Temptation of Christ is recorded in two of the Gospels - in Matthew 4 and Luke 4. Let's look at the text of both accounts side by side:

| Isaiah 52:13-15 | |
|---|---|
| **Matthew 4:1-11** | **Luke 4:1-14** |
| *Then was Jesus led up of the Spirit into the wilderness to be tempted of the devil. And when he had fasted forty days and forty nights, he was afterward an hungred.* | *And Jesus being full of the Holy Ghost returned from Jordan, and was led by the Spirit into the wilderness, Being forty days tempted of the devil. And in those days he did eat nothing: and when they were ended, he afterward hungered.* |

And when the tempter came to him, he said, If thou be the Son of God, command that these stones be made bread.

But he answered and said, It is written, Man shall not live by bread alone, but by every word that proceedeth out of the mouth of God.

Then the devil taketh him up into the holy city, and setteth him on a pinnacle of the temple,

And saith unto him, If thou be the Son of God, cast thyself down: for it is written, He shall give his angels charge concerning thee: and in their hands they shall bear thee up, lest at any time thou dash thy foot against a stone.

Jesus said unto him, It is written again, Thou shalt not tempt the Lord thy God.

Again, the devil taketh him up into an exceeding high mountain,

And the devil said unto him, If thou be the Son of God, command this stone that it be made bread.

And Jesus answered him, saying, It is written, That man shall not live by bread alone, but by every word of God.

And the devil, taking him up into an high mountain, shewed unto him all the kingdoms of the world in a moment of time.

And the devil said unto him, All this power will I give thee, and the glory of them: for that is delivered unto me; and to whomsoever I will I give it.

If thou therefore wilt worship me, all shall be thine.

And Jesus answered and said unto him, Get thee behind me, Satan: for it is written,

Thou shalt worship the Lord thy God, and him only shalt thou serve.

and sheweth him all the kingdoms of the world, and the glory of them;

And saith unto him, All these things will I give thee, if thou wilt fall down and worship me.

Then saith Jesus unto him, Get thee hence, Satan: for it is written, Thou shalt worship the Lord thy God, and him only shalt thou serve.

Then the devil leaveth him, and, behold, angels came and ministered unto him.

And he brought him to Jerusalem, and set him on a pinnacle of the temple, and said unto him, If thou be the Son of God, cast thyself down from hence:

For it is written, He shall give his angels charge over thee, to keep thee:

And in their hands they shall bear thee up, lest at any time thou dash thy foot against a stone.

And Jesus answering said unto him, It is said, Thou shalt not tempt the Lord thy God.

And when the devil had ended all the temptation, he departed from him for a season.

And Jesus returned in the power of the Spirit into Galilee: and there went out a fame of him through all the region round about.

Matthew and Luke both give us the same set of temptations. They swap the order of the second and third temptations, but the Devil makes the same three efforts in both.

It's interesting that Satan tempts Christ in three areas, and they readily fall into the categories of those worldly things listed in 1 John 2:16: "*the lust of the flesh, and the lust of the eyes, and the pride of life.*" First, Satan recognizes that Jesus has grown quite hungry after 40 days of fasting. He tempts Jesus to use His power to turn rocks into bread - appealing to the lust of the flesh. Second, Satan takes Jesus to the pinnacle of the Temple and encourages Him to leap off and let God's angels save Him. Satan is tempting Jesus to show off the power of God in Him - appealing the pride of life. Finally, Satan offers Jesus all the kingdoms of the world in return for worshipping him - appealing both to the lust of the eyes and the pride of life.

Let's look at these one at a time, using the Luke text as our base:

> *And Jesus being full of the Holy Ghost*
> *returned from Jordan, and was led by the*
> *Spirit into the wilderness, Being forty days*
> *tempted of the devil. And in those days*
> *he did eat nothing: and when they were*
> *ended, he afterward hungered.*

Luke 4:1-2

Jesus is hungry. That's no shock. A fast is tough enough for a few days, let alone 40 days. Some of us might fast cheese or red meat or movie-watching for a time, but Jesus set aside everything when He went out into the desert. He has eaten nothing for weeks. Naturally, He needs food so that He doesn't starve to death. Still, that isn't the most important matter at the moment. The most important matter is obeying God the Father:

*And the devil said unto him, If thou be the Son of God, command this stone that it be made bread. And Jesus answered him, saying, It is written, That man shall not live by bread alone, but by every word of God.*

Luke 4:3-4

We all understand who Jesus is. He is the Creator, and He could have easily snapped His fingers and produced an entire bakery there in the desert. Soon He will turn a little boy's fish and bread into a feast for more than 5000 people. This is a small thing for the Son of God, and the Devil takes advantage of Jesus' hunger to tempt Him to lose His focus on the Father.

How does Jesus respond? In each one of the temptations, Jesus answers Satan by quoting Deuteronomy. This should be a lesson for all of us. Jesus did not use philosophy with Satan. He did not explain Himself and His purposes for being out there in the desert. He simply spoke the

Word of God. When Satan tries to get Jesus to focus on His physical hunger, Jesus quotes from Deuteronomy 8. In the context there, Moses is recounting the Israelites' wandering in the desert for 40 years. This is worth noting: the people of Israel wandered and were tested in the desert for 40 years, and Jesus wandered in the desert and was tested for 40 days. Moses says:

> *And He humbled thee, and suffered thee to*
> *hunger, and fed thee with manna, which*
> *thou knewest not, neither did thy fathers*
> *know; that he might make thee know*
> *that man doth not live by bread only, but*
> *by every word that proceedeth out of the*
> *mouth of the LORD doth man live.*
>
> Deuteronomy 8:3

Jesus gets straight to the point; His life isn't about food. His life is about serving God, and for that season, God has Him in the desert fasting. That's where the Holy Spirit had led Him. His life is dependent on God's will, not on the food He eats. Rather than arguing with the Devil, Jesus speaks His answer straight from the Word of God.

He does the same when Satan makes another stab:

> *And the devil, taking him up into an*
> *high mountain, shewed unto him all the*
> *kingdoms of the world in a moment of*
> *time. And the devil said unto him,*

> *All this power will I give thee, and the*
> *glory of them: for that is delivered unto*
> *me; and to whomsoever I will I give it.*
> *If thou therefore wilt worship me, all shall*
> *be thine. And Jesus answered and said*
> *unto him, Get thee behind me, Satan:*
> *for it is written, Thou shalt worship*
> *the Lord thy God, and him only shalt*
> *thou serve.*

Luke 4:5-8

Satan shows Jesus all the kingdoms of the world in a moment. It's hard to visualize, but we can imagine it. It's interesting that Satan makes this offer and Jesus doesn't argue against his right to do so. Satan says, "*All this power will I give thee, and the glory of them.*" Satan boasts that he has the right to give kingdoms and power and glory, and Jesus doesn't deny it.

If Satan had no right to make the offer, there would have been no temptation. There's no temptation for you to do my bidding if I offer you the Sistine Chapel, because I have no rights to the Sistine Chapel. When Pilate told Jesus he had the power over His life, Jesus responded that Pilate wouldn't have any power unless it was given to him.[7] Yet, Jesus does not deny that Satan is in the position to make the offer he makes.

What did Jesus teach us to pray? "*Thy kingdom come.*" It's not until Revelation 11:15 that the seventh angel sounds his trumpet and declares: "*The kingdoms of this world are become*

23

*the kingdoms of our Lord, and of his Christ; and he shall reign for ever and ever.*" Jesus is the Messiah, and He is going to rule all the kingdoms of the world one day. Revelation 20 tells us that Satan will be bound for 1000 years, and Jesus will come to reign on the throne of David - in fulfillment of a multitude of Old Testament prophecies.[8] Before Jesus took the throne, however, He had to go through the suffering of the Cross.

Of course, Satan's offer reveals the pride and self-worship in his heart. He is ravenous for power. It echoes his desire in Isaiah 14:14 to ascend above the clouds and be "*like the Most High.*" Satan tempts Jesus with a shortcut to world domination, hoping he might actually convince the very Son of God to worship him. Instead, Jesus immediately rebukes Satan and refers to verses like Deuteronomy 5:7, 6:13-14 and 8:19 with one statement. It is unthinkable that the Son of God should worship anybody but God Himself.

Remember that Jesus came to earth as a man on our behalf, and He had to deal with the same things we all have to deal with. In the desert, the Israelites doubted God's faithfulness. They feared that the LORD had led them there to die. Here in the desert, Jesus is demonstrating His complete trust and faith in the character of the Father, and He will do things God's way always. In John 5:30, Jesus says:

*I can of mine own self do nothing:*
*as I hear, I judge: and my judgment is just;*

*because I seek not mine own will, but the
will of the Father which hath sent me.*

In the third temptation in Luke, Satan uses
Scripture himself:

*And he brought him to Jerusalem, and set
him on a pinnacle of the temple, and said
unto him, If thou be the Son of God, cast
thyself down from hence: For it is written,
He shall give his angels charge over thee,
to keep thee: And in their hands they shall
bear thee up, lest at any time thou dash thy
foot against a stone. And Jesus answering
said unto him, It is said, Thou shalt not
tempt the Lord thy God. And when the
devil had ended all the temptation, he
departed from him for a season.*

Luke 4:9-12

One of the sub-lessons here is that Satan never
hesitates to quote Scripture. He twists it for his
own diabolical purposes, but he's willing to quote
it. Here, he is goading Jesus. The King James
translates it, *"If thou be the Son of God..."* but the
connotation is, "*Since* you are the Son of God..."
There's no ambiguity about Satan's point. He's
mocking Jesus, provoking Him, trying to get Him
to prove His position by this demonstrative act.

A final time, Jesus rebuts Satan by quoting
Deuteronomy 6:16. This is where Moses is
reminding the Israelites of the events in Exodus 17,
when they tempted God because they didn't trust

Him to provide them with water. They complained and made a big commotion, because they were convinced God was going to let them die there in the desert. God gave Moses orders to strike the rock in Horeb, and water came gushing out. Moses warns them not to tempt God like that again.

Once more, Jesus demonstrates His dedication to trusting God and His plan. He does not let Satan provoke Him to prove His identity as God's Son, to force God's hand by jumping from the top of the Temple. Jesus quotes Moses, reminding Satan that it's wrong to test God through manipulation attempts. Jesus waits for the Father's timing in all things.

> *And when the devil had ended all the temptation, he departed from him for a season.*

> Luke 4:13

Satan's harassment ended then, but just for a season.

## The Prince of this World

Let's go back to the second temptation that Luke relates. Satan had the audacity to offer Jesus the kingdoms, power and glory in exchange for worshipping him. God created the world, and all things belong to Him, but it appears that Satan has a position of authority for some reason. He rules on this earth. He has many titles that should give us that understanding:

- The Prince of this World:
  John 12:31; 14:30; 16:11
- The Prince of the Power of the Air:
  Ephesians 2:2
- Head of the World Rulers of Darkness:
  Ephesians 6:12
- The god of this Age:
  2 Corinthians 4:4

Satan has power. He's got position.

Yet, his power is not unbridled. It seems he has to ask God's permission before laying a finger on one of God's own children.

# Chapter 4
# Satan in Job

What do we actually know about Satan?

His name, שָׂטָן - *Satan* - means "adversary" in Hebrew, while the Greek word for devil, διάβολος - *diabolos* - means "accuser" or "slanderer." There are some things we need to understand. Satan is a person. He's an actual individual and not just a force or the personification of evil. He has intelligence and emotion. He has a will and the ability to plan and make choices. He is morally responsible for his decisions, and everlasting fire was created to punish him and the wicked angels that followed him in his rebellion.[9] He has not always existed; he was created along with all the angels. He was originally good and beautiful, created for and by Christ. Yet some time after his creation and before Genesis 3, he rebelled against God. Jesus tells His disciples in Luke 10:18, "*I beheld Satan as lightning fall from heaven.*"

## Job

We find Satan in the oldest book of the Bible, written centuries before Moses wrote the Pentateuch. There is no mention of the Law in the book of Job, and Job serves as the priest for his family. Several centuries have passed since the

Flood, but Job still lives for another 140 years after the events of the book are over.[10] These and other pieces of internal evidence date the book of Job to the time of Abraham and the other Patriarchs.

Job opens with an extremely interesting scene. We learn that Job is a righteous family man. He has great wealth, but his major concern is that his children are clean before the LORD, so he makes sacrifices regularly on their behalf. God is impressed by Job's wholehearted devotion to what is good and upright. In fact, when Satan shows up, God singles out Job because of his righteousness.

*Now there was a day when the sons of God came to present themselves before the LORD, and Satan came also among them. And the LORD said unto Satan, Whence comest thou? Then Satan answered the LORD, and said, From going to and fro in the earth, and from walking up and down in it. And the LORD said unto Satan, Hast thou considered my servant Job, that there is none like him in the earth, a perfect and an upright man, one that feareth God, and escheweth evil?*

Job 1:6-8

We are given a rare glimpse into the heavenly realm here. Once in awhile, Scripture draws back the curtain and allows us to peek into the spiritual world. Elisha prayed for his servant in 2 Kings

6:17, asking God to open his eyes, and the servant saw the fiery chariots of protective angels crowding the hills around them. In Daniel 10 and Revelation 4 we see other hints at the goings on beyond the view of our physical eyes.

In this narrative, we find Satan entering the presence of the LORD. There are some things we should notice. First, Satan comes before the LORD among the *b'nai Elohim* - the "sons of God." This term "sons of God" always refers to direct creations of God. In this case, the sons of God are angelic beings, and in Job 38:7 we learn that they shouted for joy at the creation of the earth. Most of these angels continued to serve God, but one-third joined with Satan in rebelling against God.[11]

The Bible calls Adam a son of God because he was directly created by God, but his offspring are not direct creations - they are Adam's sons and daughters. In Genesis 6, we learn that certain of these angelic beings, these "sons of God," went down and mated with the daughters of Adam, producing the *Nephilim*, the "fallen ones."

Our adversary Satan has access to the throne room of God, and he comes to God to bring accusations against us. It's noteworthy that Satan is not omnipresent. He must go to and fro across the earth and walk "*up and down in it.*" People often make the mistake of viewing Satan as the evil-equal of God. He's not. He is a limited created being.

*Then Satan answered the LORD,*
*and said, Doth Job fear God for nought?*
*Hast not thou made an hedge about him,*
*and about his house, and about all that*
*he hath on every side? thou hast blessed*
*the work of his hands, and his substance is*
*increased in the land. But put forth thine*
*hand now, and touch all that he hath,*
*and he will curse thee to thy face.*

Job 1:9-11

Satan plays the part of the skeptic. He says, "Job's righteousness is shallow. Give him some hardship and he'll crack." God accepts Satan's challenge. In fact, He clearly set it up in the first place by drawing attention to Job. He allows Satan to destroy Job's world:

*And the LORD said unto Satan, Behold,*
*all that he hath is in thy power; only upon*
*himself put not forth thine hand. So Satan*
*went forth from the presence of the LORD.*

Job 1:12

We see here that Satan cannot touch Job without God's permission. Yet, God gives Satan leave to take everything that Job has. We know the story. In a single day, Job learns that his oxen and donkeys, his sheep and camels, his servants and all his children were wiped out in a series of invasions and freak events. It's clear that Satan can cause fire from heaven and great winds, besides leading bands of raiders to attack. He might have to walk to and fro on the earth, but he has significant power.

Satan expects Job to curse God, but Job recognizes God's sovereignty and accepts the terrible news with grace. Job's amazing response shows that Satan was wrong: man can respect God whether or not he feels materially blessed.

> *Then Job arose, and rent his mantle, and shaved his head, and fell down upon the ground, and worshipped, And said, Naked came I out of my mother's womb, and naked shall I return thither: the LORD gave, and the LORD hath taken away; blessed be the name of the LORD.*
> *In all this Job sinned not, nor charged God foolishly.*

Job 1:20-22

We understand that Satan is evil. We recognize that he hates Job and delights in doing whatever he can to get Job to curse God. Job wins, though. He humbly recognizes that everything he had was a gift from God in the first place.

In the next chapter Satan once again comes before God with the sons of God, and God asks where he's been. Again, God points out how amazing Job is, and Satan again seeks to push Job over the edge:

*And the LORD said unto Satan,*
*Hast thou considered my servant Job,*
*that there is none like him in the earth,*
*a perfect and an upright man, one that*
*feareth God, and escheweth evil? and still*
*he holdeth fast his integrity, although thou*
*movedst me against him, to destroy him*
*without cause.*

Job 2:3

God openly declares Job's innocence and recognizes the injustice performed against him. God also takes ultimate responsibility for the suffering unleashed by Satan on the righteous man. Yet, God is setting up the situation because He has a greater purpose in mind, one that will ring throughout all eternity. To this end, God goads Satan with Job.

*And Satan answered the LORD,*
*and said, Skin for skin, yea, all that a*
*man hath will he give for his life.*
*But put forth thine hand now, and touch*
*his bone and his flesh, and he will curse*
*thee to thy face. And the LORD said unto*
*Satan, Behold, he is in thine hand;*
*but save his life. So went Satan forth from*
*the presence of the LORD, and smote Job*
*with sore boils from the sole of his foot unto*
*his crown.*

Job 2:4-7

Job has lost everything, and now he is covered with painful boils. These are so dreadful that Job can do nothing but sit in an ash heap and scrape himself with a broken piece of pottery.

We know that Satan can cause physical harm. In Luke 13:10-16, Jesus heals a woman who had been bent double by a "spirit of infirmity" for 18 years, and Jesus says;

> *And ought not this woman, being a*
> *daughter of Abraham, whom Satan hath*
> *bound, lo, these eighteen years, be loosed*
> *from this bond on the sabbath day?*

Satan has the power to cause injury and disease, and he has chosen a terrible plague for Job.

The boils cover Job's entire body, including his face so that his friends cannot recognize him when they arrive in verse 2:12. He will suffer loss of appetite and depression (3:24-25); nightmares (7:14); hardened skin and running sores (7:5); difficulty in breathing (9:18); foul breath (19:17); severe weight loss and continual pain (30:17); restlessness (30:27); peeling, blackened skin and fever (30:30), all of which lasts for several months (7:3; 29:2). Even with these painful sores covering him, Job doesn't complain or speak evil of God:

> *Then said his wife unto him, Dost thou*
> *still retain thine integrity? curse God,*
> *and die. But he said unto her,*
> *Thou speakest as one of the foolish*

*women speaketh. What? shall we receive
good at the hand of God, and shall we not
receive evil? In all this did not Job sin with
his lips.*

Job 2:9-10

Notice that Satan took Job's children but left his charming wife behind.

There is a reason that God has chosen Job out of all the humans on earth. He hasn't allowed Satan to torment Job because Job has sinned. No, God chooses him because Job does love righteousness and faithfully trusts God. He does not allow Satan to torment Job forever. The suffering lasts several months, but once Job (and the rest of the world) learns the vital lessons at hand, God restores to Job double that which Satan has stolen from him.

Almost any of us would assume that God is punishing Job for something. That's the first thing we would think if somebody we knew lost everything in one day. When Job's three friends arrive to "comfort him," that's what they assume. They insist that Job must have done something to deserve his present suffering. They're completely wrong. The lesson of Job is one that speaks to all of us:

First, Job's three friends are wrong in defending their own creeds, their own theology, rather than knowing God Himself. They speak out of their own understanding rather than speaking from the heart of God. In Matthew 5:45, Jesus tells us that God, "*maketh his sun to rise on the evil and on the good, and sendeth rain on the just and on the unjust.*" In the Psalms[12] and Habakkuk, we are told not to worry when the evil man prospers, because his end is destruction. There is plenty of injustice in this world, but God makes everything right in the end.

Second, Job has defended himself to the point of considering God unjust. His view of himself is woefully inadequate, and he needs a reminder of who he is next to the all-knowing, all-powerful God of the universe.

Finally, we are in no position to judge God. God loves Job, and God has great things in store for Job. Yet, Job only has a small view of what's going on, while God understands everything perfectly. God is greater than can be described by any theology. Job doesn't understand what is happening, but God is never inconsistent, never capricious, never malicious. He is loving, and we can never forget that He sees far beyond what we see.

Job's friends are wrong to assume that God is punishing Job, but Job goes too far in his own self-defense. Starting in Chapter 38, God begins to challenge Job:

> *Then the LORD answered Job out of the whirlwind, and said, Who is this that darkeneth counsel by words without knowledge? Gird up now thy loins like*

*a man; for I will demand of thee,*
*and answer thou me. Where wast thou*
*when I laid the foundations of the earth?*
*declare, if thou hast understanding.*

Job 38:1-4

Job has gotten a little big for his britches, and God nips that attitude. He challenges human wisdom. Interestingly enough, God starts with the origin of the earth itself. He challenges Job to tell Him where he was when the earth was formed. The obvious answer is that Job wasn't born yet. God continues, asking Job to tell Him how the earth was made. Of course, Job can't explain anything about it because he wasn't there:

*Who hath laid the measures thereof,*
*if thou knowest? or who hath stretched*
*the line upon it? Whereupon are the*
*foundations thereof fastened? or who laid*
*the corner stone thereof; When the morning*
*stars sang together, and all the sons of God*
*shouted for joy?*

Job 38:5-7

We saw the phrase "sons of God" in chapters 1 and 2, and here we see this phrase again. These are the angels. The Septuagint makes it easy for us to know they are angels, because it translates the Hebrew "son of God" into the Greek term "angels" so there's no confusion. The angels were there when God made the earth. They witnessed the creation of the world of humankind, and they rejoiced! This means that the angels were already in existence themselves.

Satan was one of the direct creations of God. He was one of the *benai Elohim*, the sons of God - the angels. This means that Satan was around and able to watch God create the earth.

God spends chapters 38-42 making His point, and Job realizes that his attitude needs some adjustment.

> *Then Job answered the LORD, and said,*
> *I know that thou canst do every thing,*
> *and that no thought can be withholden*
> *from thee. … I have heard of thee by the*
> *hearing of the ear: but now mine eye seeth*
> *thee. Wherefore I abhor myself, and repent*
> *in dust and ashes.*

Job 42:1-2, 5-6

Job does what Satan refuses to do. Job lays aside his pride, and he recognizes the preeminence of the God who created all things. He had heard of God, but now he sees Him, and his only response to God's glory is to repent and humble himself in His presence.

There's something more we can gather from God's challenge to Job in chapter 38, however. We begin to get some clues about what happened in the spiritual realm before corrupted Satan appeared in Genesis 3.

# Chapter 5
# The Cosmos

God takes time to challenge Job about the creation of the world, and He gives us some interesting descriptions as He does so. He asks Job:

> *...Or who shut up the sea with doors,*
> *when it brake forth, as if it had issued*
> *out of the womb? When I made the cloud*
> *the garment thereof, and thick darkness*
> *a swaddlingband for it. And brake up*
> *for it my decreed place, and set bars and*
> *doors, And said, Hitherto shalt thou come,*
> *but no further: and here shall thy proud*
> *waves be stayed? Hast thou commanded*
> *the morning since thy days; and caused the*
> *dayspring to know his place; That it might*
> *take hold of the ends of the earth, that*
> *the wicked might be shaken out of it? It is*
> *turned as clay to the seal; and they stand*
> *as a garment. And from the wicked their*
> *light is withholden, and the high arm shall*
> *be broken.*

Job 38:8-15

God talks about forming the oceans and making them to stay in one place, which sounds like the third day of Creation. He talks about commanding the morning, which sounds like the first day of Creation. When did all this happen? What is God talking about here? We recognize that this is poetic language, but it might be alluding to something very specific. We see an original creation here, and perhaps a judgment as well.

Ultimately, we know that the angels were created before the earth. We also know that Satan had already fallen by Genesis 3.

The question that lurks behind the text is … when did Satan fall? We will learn in a few pages that he was the highest of the angels. He had charge of all the other angels, but he coveted the position of greatest authority, that of God Himself. Satan's pride ended in his judgment.

When did that take place?

It couldn't have happened before Genesis 1:1, because that was the beginning of everything. "*In the beginning, God created the heavens and the earth.*" That's all inclusive. By Genesis 3, Satan's heavenly position had been taken from him. So we find a question there: when did Satan fall, and how did he gain his position of power that he boasts about in the temptations of Christ?

### The Cosmos

We're dealing here with the cosmos. Puny man finds himself in the middle of this enormous, vast universe. We need to expand from puny to large, from man to the Earth, the solar system, to the greater universe. This is the world explored by the field of science we call astronomy or astrophysics. It's the macrocosm of our world, the big side of things.

One of the discoveries of 20th century science is that the universe is finite. It has an edge. It also appears to be expanding, which leads to all these conjectures about the Big Bang. If it's expanding, then there was a point at which everything was much closer together, which assumes a beginning point of expansion. We will get back to what God's Word says about Satan, but I want to take a moment for us to shed the baggage of our presuppositions about the universe. We often encumber our understanding because incorrect preconceptions stand in the way.

### The Nebular Hypothesis

How did our solar system form? The basic explanation is what's called the Nebular Hypothesis, which can be summarized as follows: "About 4.5 billion years ago, the sun ejected a tail, a filament of material that cooled and collected into balls of matter that formed the planets." This is the basic view taught to most astronomy students.

The Nebular Hypothesis is generally credited to the great astronomer Immanuel Kant, but it was actually first offered by a mining engineer named Emanuel Swedenborg (1688-1772). In 1734, Swedenborg published *Prodromus Philosophiae Retiocinantis de Infinito et Cause*

*Creationis* in Latin, in which he describes the formation of the solar system from the spinning solar nebula. Swedenborg spent a lot of time around astronomers like Edmond Halley, after whom the famous comet is named. Swedenborg also had some strange spiritual practices. He claimed to have psychic powers, and he allegedly communicated with beings on Jupiter and Saturn and other planets through séances. His books *Arcana Coelestia* (1749-1756) and *Earths in the Universe* (1758) describe some of the discussions with these other spiritual beings. Many of his theological ideas came from these "angels" on other planets, but they were ideas that contradicted the straight-forward interpretation of the Scriptures. For instance, he regarded the books of Moses as symbolic, representing our own individual struggles, rather than the literal history of the Hebrew people.

Swedenborg claimed to be a Christian who served Jesus Christ, and he managed to impress people by his visions. For instance, he allegedly described a fire taking place in Stockholm on July 19, 1759, even though it took several days for news of the fire to reach Gothenburg where he was staying.[13] We are warned in 1 John 4:1 to test the spirits, however, because false prophets have gone into the world. Swedenborg might very well have been in communication with other spiritual beings, but they led him into some very bad theology.

Swedenborg did have some astronomical knowledge due to his friendship with Edmond Halley. When Swedenborg was 23 years old, he spent several weeks at Halley's home. This gave Swedenborg some astronomy background to beef up his alternative ideas about the origin of the solar system.

Immanuel Kant went back and forth between admiring and demonizing Swedenborg, but Kant finally embraced Swedenborg's ideas. Twenty years after Swedenborg's *Prodromus*, Kant published his *General History of Nature and Theory of the Heavens* (1755), in which he describes the Nebular Hypothesis. The mathematician Pierre Laplace gave his approval to the idea as well, which encouraged its wide-spread acceptance. The problem is that both of these scientists failed to expose the mathematical problems with the Nebular Hypothesis, to their shame. It appears clear they did not sufficiently double-check the math before adding their seal of approval to this very faulty theory.

Unfortunately, the Nebular Hypothesis has taken its undeserved place in the halls of scientific respectability. Rather than throwing out the idea, modern astronomers have merely worked to explain away its many problems. Let's look at a few of them:

## Nebular Troubles

### *The Planets have all the Angular Momentum:*

The Sun contains almost all of the solar system's mass - 99.87% of it. The Sun's mass of $1.99 \times 10^{30}$ kg is more than 745 times the combined mass of all the planets. Yet, the Sun contains less than 4% of the angular momentum of the solar system. That doesn't make sense.

| Planet | Mass (kg) | Orbital Ang. Moment. (kg m2/sec) | % of Solar System Orb Ang. Moment. |
|--------|-----------|----------------------------------|------------------------------------|
| Mercury | $3.30 \times 10^{23}$ | $9.1 \times 10^{38}$ | 0.003% |
| Venus | $4.87 \times 10^{24}$ | $1.8 \times 10^{40}$ | 0.058% |
| Earth | $5.97 \times 10^{24}$ | $2.7 \times 10^{40}$ | 0.087% |
| Mars | $6.42 \times 10^{23}$ | $3.5 \times 10^{39}$ | 0.011% |
| Jupiter | $1.90 \times 10^{27}$ | $1.9 \times 10^{43}$ | 61.2% |
| Saturn | $5.68 \times 10^{26}$ | $7.8 \times 10^{42}$ | 25.1% |
| Uranus | $8.68 \times 10^{25}$ | $1.7 \times 10^{42}$ | 5.48% |
| Neptune | $1.02 \times 10^{26}$ | $2.5 \times 10^{42}$ | 8.05% |
| | Total: $2.67 \times 10^{27}$ | Total: $3.1 \times 10^{43}$ | |

If nebular dust collapsed into a fiery ball, creating the Sun, it should have spun faster as its diameter got smaller (as the ball grew denser) - just as ice skaters spin faster as they make themselves more compact. Yet, the angular momentum is concentrated in the orbital angular momentum of the planets outside the Sun, while the Sun itself spins at a much slower rate.

### *Discordant Momentum of Planets v. Moons:*

If the Nebular Hypothesis were true, we'd expect to see a correlation between the angular momentum of the various planets and their moons. The combined orbital momentum of all the planets is about 28 times larger than the Sun's angular momentum, yet Earth's moon has an orbital angular momentum that's only four times greater than Earth's rotational angular momentum. Jupiter's situation is completely different; its rotational momentum is nearly 154 times larger than the orbital angular momentum of its four largest moons. If the planets all formed from the same spinning nebular material, we should not only see mathematical relationships between the angular momentum of the planets and the Sun, we should also see a relationship between the momentum of the planets and their moons. We don't see any such thing. We don't see the mathematical harmony we'd expect.

The four largest moons of Jupiter were known by Galileo as early as 1610. These things could have been checked by Laplace in his day, but he and Kant embraced a weak hypothesis before thoroughly vetting it.

| Name | Mass (kg) | Rotational Ang. Moment. (kg m2/sec) | Orbital Ang. Momentum of Satellites (kg m2/sec) | Rotational/ Orbital momentum |
|------|-----------|-------------------------------------|--------------------------------------------------|-------------------------------|
| Sun | $1.99 \times 10^{30}$ | $1.1 \times 10^{42}$ | (planets) $3.1 \times 10^{43}$ | 1/28 |
| Earth | $5.97 \times 10^{24}$ | $7.1 \times 10^{33}$ | (moon) $2.9 \times 10^{34}$ | 1/4 |
| Jupiter | $1.90 \times 10^{27}$ | $6.9 \times 10^{38}$ | (moons) $4.49 \times 10^{36}$ | 153 2/3 |

## *Spin Rates and Axial Tilts Vary:*

We find a bizarre range of spinning rates and axial tilts among the planets, when we would expect them to all spin at a similar rate relative to their masses. Three sets of planets appear to be paired up. Earth and Mars both have a day-length of about 24 hours. Jupiter and Saturn are spinning much faster, especially relative to their enormous size, and both have a day-length of about 10 hours. Neptune and Uranus each rotate once on their axes every 16-17 hours. Mercury and Venus are the odd bodies. Mercury spins once every 59 Earth days, and Venus rotates so slowly that its year (224.7 Earth days) is shorter than its day (243 Earth days).

Earth and Mars also have a nearly identical axial tilt. Earth is tilted at 23.5° and Mars at 25.2°. Jupiter and Saturn are no longer equals here, though. Saturn and Neptune, each on opposite sides of Uranus, have tilts of about 27° and 28° respectively, while Jupiter and Mercury have hardly any tilt at all. Venus is extremely strange. It has nearly no tilt and it has retrograde rotation. That is, the Sun rises (slowly) in the west and sets in the east on Venus. It is therefore considered to be upside-down and its tilt is labelled 177° (nearly 180°). Uranus lies almost directly on its side, and its rotation is considered retrograde like Venus' because its tilt is greater than 90°. Uranus' largest moons are tilted at about 98°. Astronomers are still trying to figure out how the planet tilts and spin rates came to be, since these do not fit what we'd expect from the Nebular Hypothesis.

| Planet | Rotation | Axial Tilt (degrees) | Density (g/cm3) |
|--------|----------|----------------------|------------------|
| Mercury | 58.79 days | 0 | 5.427 |
| Venus | 243.69 days | 177.36 | 5.243 |
| Earth | 23.93 hours | 23.45 | 5.515 |
| Mars | 24.62 hours | 25.19 | 3.933 |
| Jupiter | 9.93 hours | 3.13 | 1.326 |
| Saturn | 10.66 hours | 26.73 | 0.687 |
| Uranus | 17.24 hours | 97.77 | 1.270 |
| Neptune | 16.11 hours | 28.32 | 1.638 |

## *Outer Planets are Biggest:*

There are other facts that don't fit the standard theory. Classic mathematician James Jeans (1877-1946) first made note that the outer planets are much larger than the inner ones. Jupiter is almost 6,000 times as massive as Mercury and nearly 3,000 times more massive than Mars. We'd expect the largest amount of material to have remained near the Sun. Modern defenders of the updated Nebular Hypothesis argue that the inner planets are made up of the small amounts of silica and metals that could bear the heat near the Sun, while the outer gas giants are made of the larger amounts of everything else.

As cosmologists recognized some of these difficulties during the 20th century, the Nebular Hypothesis began losing its following. Soviet astronomer Victor Safronov attempted to answer several problems by offering his solar nebular disk model (SNDM) in his 1972 book, *Evolution of the Protoplanetary Cloud and Formation of the Earth and the Planets*. He couldn't provide explanations for everything, especially the axial tilt issue, and astronomers still readily admit there are unanswered puzzles.

### *Oxygen Levels Don't Match:*

Despite Safronov's brave efforts, additional problems with the Nebular Hypothesis continue to show up. NASA's 2004 Genesis mission collected solar wind debris and the researchers were surprised to find that oxygen levels were much higher in the Sun than elsewhere. O-16 is the most common oxygen isotope, but it is apparently far denser in the Sun than in Earth or Mars or the moon.[14] Researcher Kevin McKeegan told *Space Daily*:

> We found that Earth, the moon, as well as Martian and other meteorites which are samples of asteroids, have a lower concentration of the O-16 than does the sun…The implication is that we did not form out of the same solar

nebula materials that created the sun - just how and why remains to be discovered.[15]

The long-held favoring of the Nebular Hypothesis and its modern variants makes me think of a scene from Lewis Carroll's book *Through The Looking Glass*:

> "I can't believe that!" said Alice.
> "Can't you?" the Queen said in a pitying tone. "Try again: draw a long breath, and shut your eyes."
> Alice laughed. "There's no use trying," she said: "one *can't* believe impossible things."
> "I daresay you haven't had much practice," said the Queen. "When I was your age, I always did it for half-an-hour a day. Why, sometimes I've believed as many as six impossible things before breakfast."

We can get good at believing impossible things without even realizing it.

# Chapter 6
# Our Rough Neighborhood

There are certain things we can tell by studying the planets today. For instance, it's clear that the solar system was a violent place at times in its history. A full 93% of Mars' craters are on one side of the red planet and appear to have been made in a single eight-hour period. We don't even need a telescope to see that our own moon is terribly beat up. The face of the "man on the moon" is the result of cosmic battering.

When trying to piece together what happened in the past, geologists and astronomers must fall into one of two categories. If they assume that processes have remained largely the same for the past billions of years, then they are called uniformitarians. Earth has obviously changed, but uniformitarians argue it does so slowly and steadily over large blocks of time according to the same processes we see today. Their motto is, "The present is the key to the past."

Catastrophists see things in the opposite light. They believe Earth, the solar system and the universe have been subjected to various catastrophic events. Catastrophists try to infer what's happened in one after another of a series of disasters over the years. Creationists tend to fall into this second category.

The Moon has offered Earth much protection, but our blue planet still shows evidence of more than 100 large impacts. A giant meteor hits us every 300 years or so. Two-thirds of these land in the ocean, but some very serious rocks have slammed into the ground. An impact crater near Winslow, Arizona gouged a hole in the earth one mile wide. The famous crater on the Yucatan Peninsula is an inconceivable six miles in diameter. The explosion from that particular impact equaled the destruction of a 100-megaton bomb.

On June 30, 1908 near the Tunguska River in northern Siberia, a meteor crashed and left a crater 400 yards in diameter. It was so remote from civilization, it wasn't explored until 17 years after the fact in 1925. The impact was equivalent to a 15-megaton nuclear warhead.

**Mars**

Do you know what the Muslims worship at the Ka'aba? A meteorite landed in what is now the city of Mecca in Saudi Arabia. Two thousand years before Muhammad, the people created the Ka'aba in its honor. Cairo in Egypt is the site of the great pyramids, and it's interesting that "Cairo" is believed to have been derived from the Arabic name for Mars "Al Najm Al Qahir." In Acts 17, Paul climbs up on the Areopagus - Mars Hill - in Athens to talk to the people.

Mars was the Roman god of war. He was the Baal of the Old Testament, a menacing god to be feared. There aren't many of us who could even point out Mars in the night sky if we had to, yet the ancient people revered and feared Mars. Today Mars is a small red dot, if we look carefully. But it appears Mars once passed much closer to Earth than it does today.

Earth and Mars have an interesting relationship. Their tilts are similar. Their day-lengths are similar. It's suspected that their orbits were also in harmony early in Earth's history; Earth's orbit was 360 days and Mars' orbit was 720 days. Their orbits would have been in resonance, like tuning forks - harmonic in their revolution around the Sun.

If we model this, we find that they would have passed by each other much more closely than they do today, which means their gravitational pulls on each other would have caused major geological episodes. In fact, their near pass-by periods offer an explanation for major catastrophic events throughout ancient history every 700 years or so.

It's clear that something exceptional took place in 701 B.C. - an event so extreme that it added several more days to Earth's year and threw off the harmony between Earth and its red neighbor. The calendars of all major civilizations changed at that point. While the calendars had operated according to a 360-day year, they had to adjust. The Jews decided to add one extra month seven times every 19 years. The Romans added 5 ¼ days per year. Something had to be done to account for the new additional days.

Today, Earth has a solar year of 365 ¼ days and Mars has a year of 687 days. Their orbits no longer closely resonate, and the two planets no longer pass closely to each other as they did thousands of years ago, but the evidence for this ancient harmony can be seen in the fear the ancients had of the red planet.

Things are not the same today as they were in the past. The solar system today has changed from what it was.

## The Moons of Mars

Mars has two tiny, nearly invisible moons. Despite the great interest in astronomy in the 16th and 17th centuries, it took until 1877 for Asaph Hall to finally find these two dark moons of Mars using a new telescope at the U.S. Naval Observatory. There are a couple of different facts that make these two moons extremely interesting. One is that Jonathan Swift wrote about them in his book *Gulliver's Travels* in 1726, 151 years before modern science knew they existed.

How did Jonathan Swift do that? Good question.

We think of *Gulliver's Travels* as a set of children's stories, but they were actually written as political satires making fun of 18th century England. We're familiar with the little people of Lilliput, but in Gulliver's third voyage, he visits a place called Laputa. Laputa is a land of scientists, who insult of the astronomers in London because they don't know about the two moons of Mars.

It's just a story. However, the details that Swift gives about the two moons of Mars are much closer to reality than mere guesswork should have ever produced.

We now know that Mars' moon Deimos is less than 8 miles in diameter and it's second moon, Phobos, is not much larger - only about 14 miles across. Phobos is the nearer moon to Mars and Deimos is the moon farther out. Both moons have an exceptionally low reflectivity, and Phobos is the darkest thing in our solar system, reflecting only about 3% of the light that hits it. Both Martian moons rotate so that the same side always faces Mars. Deimos revolves around Mars once every 30 hours and 18 minutes, which is exceptionally fast. In comparison, our Moon takes 29 ½ days to revolve around the Earth. Phobos zooms around Mars even faster than Deimos, making its circuit once every 7.65 hours. Phobos also defies all the other moons in our solar system by taking its trip around Mars backwards.

In chapter three of the *Voyage To Laputa*, Swift describes the two moon of Mars as follows:

They have likewise discovered two lesser stars, or satellites, which revolve about Mars; whereof the innermost is distant from the center of the primary planet exactly three of his diameters, and the outermost, five; the former revolves in the space of ten hours, and the latter in twenty-one and a half; so that the squares of their periodical times are very near the same proportion with the cubes of their distance from the center of Mars; which evidently shows them to be governed by the same law of gravitation that influences the other heavenly bodies.

Swift was friendly with the astronomers of his day. He knew Newton, Halley, and Winston personally, and he could have made calculations about the moons' periodical times based on Kepler Laws of Motion. Swift's descriptions of Phobos and Deimos are not precise; Phobos circles the planet in 7 hours and 39 minutes, not 10 hours, but Swift's details are bizarrely close. He describes *two* moons - not one or four. What's more, Phobos has been pulling closer to Mars at a rate of 1.8m every century, which means that its orbit would have been longer in the distant past.

It's possible that Jonathan Swift had access to myths or legends, and he made use of them and tossed in Kepler's laws for the fun of it. He likely had no idea how close his sources were to the truth. It would have been impossible for anybody to see those moons prior to the invention of powerful telescopes. That is, unless Mars passed very close to the Earth in the distant past.

Mars would have had to approach Earth at a range of merely 70-80,000 miles for any ancient peoples to see its moons with the naked eye. At that distance, Mars would have loomed huge and terrifying in the sky, 50 times the size of our Moon. October 25th 1404 BC, the pass by would have caused severe earthquakes and land tides, and a polar shift of about 5 degrees would have lengthened the day - just in time for Joshua to fight Adonizedek at Beth Horon in Joshua 10. It's not a miracle that meteors fell - flying through the sky at 30,000 miles per hour. It's a miracle that those great stones from the sky hit only the fleeing enemies of Israel.

The world has changed greatly throughout its history. We cannot base our views on the ancient past based on today's version of "normal."

All this is leading up to a particular catastrophe, a specific time of destruction that took place at the very beginning, between the first and second verses of Genesis.

# Chapter 7
# A Gap Theory

There are two kinds of people that deal with the Gap Theory - those that dismiss it as nonsense, or those that misapply it. We'll try to do neither. I simply want to bring understanding to a particular interval in between the first two verses of Genesis.

When were the angels created? When did Satan fall? That's the issue before us:

*In the beginning God created the heaven and the earth.*

Genesis 1:1

Period. If we accept that first statement, we should have no problem with any other verse in the Bible. That says it all. There's no contest.

*And the earth was without form, and void; and darkness was upon the face of the deep. And the Spirit of God moved upon the face of the waters. And God said, Let there be light: and there was light.*

Genesis 1:2-3

Let's focus on the second verse, which tells us that the earth was without form and void.

The Hebrew term is תהו ובהו - *tohu v'bohu* -
"formless and void." Interestingly, there is a verse
in Isaiah that seems to contradict this. In Isaiah
45:18, God says, "*For thus saith the LORD that
created the heavens; God himself that formed the
earth and made it; he hath established it, he created
it not in vain...*"

God says, "I didn't create it formless and
void." He didn't create it in vain; He formed it
to be inhabited.

Of course, any time we find what appears
to be a contradiction in the Bible, we should
rejoice, because there's always a treasure there to
be discovered.

Let's look further. We find Jeremiah crying
out in grief over the impending destruction of
Jerusalem. Then, in Jeremiah 4, he says something
very interesting:

*I beheld the earth, and, lo, it was without
form, and void; and the heavens, and they
had no light. I beheld the mountains, and,
lo, they trembled, and all the hills moved
lightly. I beheld, and, lo, there was no
man, and all the birds of the heavens were
fled. I beheld, and, lo, the fruitful place
was a wilderness, and all the cities thereof
were broken down at the presence of the
LORD, and by his fierce anger. For thus
hath the LORD said, The whole land shall
be desolate; yet will I not make a full end.*
                                  Jeremiah 4:23-27

This is clearly a time of judgment. Notice that Jeremiah uses the terms *tohu v'bohu* again - "formless and void." The heavens hold no light. It's as though the world has returned to the chaos that existed before Creation Week.

Why isn't God making a full end? He must have a plan in mind. As we poke around in Scripture, we see other interesting verses:

> *Then the earth shook and trembled;*
> *the foundations also of the hills moved*
> *and were shaken, because he was wroth.*
> *There went up a smoke out of his nostrils,*
> *and fire out of his mouth devoured:*
> *coals were kindled by it. He bowed*
> *the heavens also, and came down:*
> *and darkness was under his feet. And he*
> *rode upon a cherub, and did fly: yea,*
> *he did fly upon the wings of the wind.*
> *He made darkness his secret place; his*
> *pavilion round about him were dark*
> *waters and thick clouds of the skies.*
> *At the brightness that was before him his*
> *thick clouds passed, hail stones and coals*
> *of fire. The LORD also thundered in the*
> *heavens, and the Highest gave his voice;*
> *hail stones and coals of fire. Yea, he sent*
> *out his arrows, and scattered them; and he*
> *shot out lightnings, and discomfited them.*
> *Then the channels of waters were seen,*
> *and the foundations of the world were*

*discovered at thy rebuke, O LORD,*
*at the blast of the breath of thy nostrils.*

Psalm 18:7-15

Maybe this is just flowery language. David is praising God for His protection and for saving him from his enemies, so we might regard this as David's hyperbole in portraying God's passion in rescuing him. On the other hand, David is a prophet and this sounds like a cosmic judgment. The poet describes earthquakes and fire, hailstones and brimstone and lightning. The very earth is torn open letting loose channels of water. This is serious business, and it might hearken back to actual events in Earth's history. If so, when did these world-shaking episodes take place?

Genesis 1:2 offers a key. The King James translates it, "*And the earth was without form, and void, and darkness was upon the face of the deep.*" The first word translated "was" in this verse is היה - *hayah* - in its feminine perfect form היתה, indicating something that is completed – a change has been made. It is the same verb form Moses used in Exodus 9:24 to say Egypt "became" a nation. In other words, the earth *became* without form and void.

Furthermore, there is a conjunction just before *hayah*. The conjunction is the single letter *vav*, translated "and." It is an adversative conjunction, meaning it should actually be considered "but" or "however," which is how the Latin Vulgate translates it. That "however" indicates a time delay. The first part of Genesis 1:2 is therefore better translated thus:

"*But the earth became formless and void…*"

Something happened between verses 1 and 2. It appears there was a judgment that resulted in the formless chaos.

"*And darkness was upon the face of the deep.*"

This darkness is not just the absence of light; it's an unnatural darkness. This is the darkness that falls on the Egyptians in Exodus 10:22. In the Greek, "the deep" is translated "the abyss" - the bottomless pit. This abyss is the home of the demons and evil spirits that pour out in Revelation 9.

So, God created the heavens and the earth. Then, something happened that the earth became without form and void, and now darkness is on the face of the deep. One of the hypotheses we want to explore here is that there was a usurper, a traitor, and his judgment resulted in some changes.

This is one gap theory, and as far as I can tell it was first suggested by Thomas Chalmers (1780-1847) in a lecture in 1814. In his writings, he said simply, "The detailed history of creation in the first chapter of Genesis begins at the middle of the second verse."[16] The classic book on this subject is George Pember's book, *Earth's Earliest Ages* originally published 1884 and readily available in most bookstores. One of my must-reads is

*The Invisible War* by Donald Grey Barnhouse. It's a fabulous book on this whole subject. I also recommend *Without Form and Void* by Arthur Custance.

It appears there was a judgment resulting in chaos early on, before Creation Week began. This has nothing to do with geological ages. It does give us an idea about destruction in the heavenlies - and why we find a vindictive serpent creeping through the Garden of Eden soon after the creation of humans.

# Chapter 8
# The King of Tyre

We cannot find a single chapter in the Bible that explains to us the exact events surrounding the fall of Satan. We have to collect the bits of information hidden here and there throughout the Bible. Ezekiel 28 is a treasure trove in that respect, because God speaks to the power that's behind the throne of Tyre. Let's look what Ezekiel says:

> *The word of the LORD came again unto me, saying, Son of man, say unto the prince of Tyrus, Thus saith the Lord GOD; Because thine heart is lifted up, and thou hast said, I am a God, I sit in the seat of God, in the midst of the seas; yet thou art a man, and not God, though thou set thine heart as the heart of God:*

Ezekiel 28:1-2

God speaks to Ezekiel about the prince of Tyre, who is an egomaniac. This is clearly the political leader in charge of the city of Tyre, situated on the Mediterranean coast north of Israel. He was ruler of the "holy" island of Tyre, which was considered at the time to have risen from the rock throne of God, and he had too high a view of himself.

This prince is a man, but he thinks he's God. He's deluded. He's been so intoxicated by his own power, he's forgotten his own humanity.

Pharaoh has the same problem in Ezekiel 29, boasting that he's made the Nile River for himself. Herod Agrippa accepts worship at the end of Acts 12, which results in God's judgment against him; he is "eaten of worms" and dies. In 2 Thessalonians 2:3-4, we find that the "man of sin" will sit in the Temple of God accepting worship, exalting himself above everything that is called God, portraying himself as God.

Here in Ezekiel 28, God says to the prince of Tyre, "…*though thou set thine heart as the heart of God.*" The words remind us of the temptation in Genesis 3:5: "*ye shall be as gods...*" The prince of Tyre is not God. He's just swollen up with his own self-worship.

*Behold, thou art wiser than Daniel;*
*there is no secret that they can hide from*
*thee: With thy wisdom and with thine*
*understanding thou hast gotten thee riches,*
*and hast gotten gold and silver into thy*
*treasures: By thy great wisdom and by*
*thy traffick hast thou increased thy riches,*
*and thine heart is lifted up because of*
*thy riches:*

Ezekiel 28:3-5

We can hear the sarcasm here. The prince of Tyre thinks he knows everything. He's gotten rich, and he gives all the glory to himself for it. There are many people who have worked very hard and made wise decisions, yet they barely scrape by. There are others who just seem blessed with the Midas touch. Riches flow to them, and it's easy for them to think it's all because of how great *they* are. That's the folly of the prince of Tyre. He thinks he's the smartest thing in the world, having created riches through his own brilliance, and his ego is ridiculously swollen because of it. Yet, we know that God resists the proud and gives grace to the humble.[17] We also know that pride comes before destruction.[18]

> *Therefore thus saith the Lord GOD;*
> *Because thou hast set thine heart as the*
> *heart of God; Behold, therefore I will bring*
> *strangers upon thee, the terrible of the*
> *nations: and they shall draw their swords*
> *against the beauty of thy wisdom, and*
> *they shall defile thy brightness. They shall*
> *bring thee down to the pit, and thou shalt*
> *die the deaths of them that are slain in the*
> *midst of the seas. Wilt thou yet say before*
> *him that slayeth thee, I am God? but thou*
> *shalt be a man, and no God, in the hand*
> *of him that slayeth thee. Thou shalt die the*
> *deaths of the uncircumcised by the hand*
> *of strangers: for I have spoken it, saith the*
> *Lord GOD.*

Ezekiel 28:6-10

Here, God tells the prince of Tyre, "You think you are a god. The guy that cuts off your head won't be too impressed." Because of his great arrogance and self-worship, the man sitting on the throne of Tyre will be conquered and killed. In the 6th century, Nebuchadnezzar came in and besieged Tyre during the reign of Ithobaal III. This wealthy leader of Tyre was removed from his throne by Nebuchadnezzar, and his name has been largely washed away from history. Most of us are familiar with the identity of Nebuchadnezzar. Few people have ever heard of Ithobaal III. So much for his claim to be God.

At this point in Ezekiel 28, though, the language starts to shift strangely. God deals with the prince of Tyre in the first 10 verses, but then He seems to move beyond the foolish egomaniac sitting physically on the throne of Tyre to the *spiritual* ruler of Tyre. God even changes titles. In the first 10 verses, He addresses the "prince" of Tyre, the *nagid.* In the next section, however, He will speak to the *melech,* the "king" of Tyre.

> *Moreover the word of the LORD came unto me, saying, Son of man, take up a lamentation upon the king of Tyrus, and say unto him, Thus saith the Lord GOD; Thou sealest up the sum, full of wisdom, and perfect in beauty.*

Ezekiel 28:11-12

Notice that it doesn't say he *thinks* he is perfect in beauty. It appears that this "king of Tyre" actually *is* the most beautiful thing. He is full of wisdom. In fact, he sealed up the sum in these things - there was nobody better. That is, until iniquity was found in him. The language here is similar to the language God uses toward the king of Babylon in Isaiah 14, where this being is called "Lucifer."

We find that the antichrist embodies these things. In Daniel 7, he is the little horn speaking great things, who subdues three kingdoms. In Revelation 13:2, the dragon gives him great power and authority. Look how God describes him next, though:

> *Thou hast been in Eden the garden of God;*
> *every precious stone was thy covering, the*
> *sardius, topaz, and the diamond, the beryl,*
> *the onyx, and the jasper, the sapphire,*
> *the emerald, and the carbuncle, and gold:*
> *the workmanship of thy tabrets and of thy*
> *pipes was prepared in thee in the day that*
> *thou wast created.*

Ezekiel 28:13

Eden. That's going back a little bit. Adam and Eve were kicked out of Eden in Genesis 3, and the way was guarded by cherubim and a flaming sword. Clearly the human leader of Tyre had never been in Eden. The spiritual power behind the throne of Tyre, however, was not just in Eden, but he was clothed in great beauty. Every precious stone covered him. He was given well-crafted musical instruments in the day he was created.

This created being summed up what it meant to be beautiful. He was made full of beauty and wisdom, and nobody surpassed him. Yet, he was still a creation.

He was covered with every precious stone - diamonds and sapphires, emeralds and gold. Can we imagine a being more glorious, with light sparkling off the multitude of colorful gems that covered him? These stones listed here are among the same stones that emblazoned the high priest's breastplate. Exodus 28:15-21 gives instruction for making this breastplate, and the stones were to be placed in four rows of three. The first stone listed is the sardius. It was the stone of Reuben, whose name means "behold the son." The last stone listed in Exodus 28 is the jasper, which represents Benjamin, "the son of my right hand." These become the bookends of the 12 tribes, from the first to the last. They are also both titles of Christ: "behold the son" and "the son of my right hand."

It's interesting that here in Ezekiel 28, only nine of these precious stones are listed in the Hebrew Masoretic Text. That is, all the breastplate gems are listed in Ezekiel 28, except that the gems from the breastplate's third row are missing. On the other hand, all 12 are listed in the

Septuagint, so apparently somebody accidentally dropped out a portion of the text during the 900 years from the Septuagint translation to the most recent Masoretic Text version.

We recognize that a most beautiful array of gems garnished the clothing of this glorious created being found in the Garden of Eden. I'm going to take the liberty of calling him "Lucifer" here, as he is called in Isaiah 14.

He was the top of everything. God also refers to "*the workmanship of thy tabrets and of thy pipes.*" Those are musical instruments like tambourines or flutes. This is why many people believe that Lucifer's skill at music was unexcelled. Many people presume that he was the leader of the worship in heaven.

> *Thou art the anointed cherub that covereth; and I have set thee so: thou wast upon the holy mountain of God; thou hast walked up and down in the midst of the stones of fire. Thou wast perfect in thy ways from the day that thou wast created, till iniquity was found in thee.*
>
> Ezekiel 28:14-15

He is called here "*the anointed cherub.*" The word *cherub* is singular, and *cherubim* is plural. The cherubim are the super angels, the powerful, holy angels that surround the throne of God. Cherubim were sent to guard the way into the Garden of Eden. Golden likenesses of cherubim were formed on the Ark of the Covenant, with their wings extended over the mercy seat, according to God's instructions in Exodus 25:18-22. God spoke to Moses from between the cherubim in the tabernacle, just as He spoke to Ezekiel from the midst of the real cherubim in Ezekiel 10.

Here we find that Lucifer is the anointed cherub. That's an incredible position of honor. Kings are anointed and thus appointed and blessed by God to take their places as rulers. Lucifer is the anointed cherub who was given authority and mandate to run things.

God placed Lucifer on the holy mountain of God, where he walked amidst the stones of fire. In prophesy, a mountain idiomatically represents a government. The rock that is Christ's kingdom strikes the statue of world governments in Daniel 2 and becomes a mountain that fills the entire earth. Lucifer was on God's holy mountain, and he was created perfect. His ways were perfect - until he allowed iniquity to enter him. That is the sad part. He allowed sin to creep into his heart, and Lucifer the morning star became Satan the adversary.

Christ created Lucifer. John 1:3 and Colossians 1:16 tell us that all things were made by and for Christ, which includes this glorious and beautiful super angel. This is important to appreciate. Satan, even with all his powers, is still only Christ's handiwork. There's no contest between Satan and Christ, because Jesus Christ is the Creator, while Satan is His creation.

The real mystery here is why God didn't just snuff out Satan. God is not the author of sin, and He did not place pride and rebellion into Lucifer's heart. Lucifer managed that all on his own. Yet, God let Lucifer's rebellion play out. Why? Because even in his desire to destroy God's creation, Satan inadvertently fulfills God's agenda of salvation for eternity. Throughout the ages, any number of created beings might have allowed pride and rebellion to infest their souls like a cancer, polluting the universe. God allowed the wages of sin to play out, and then He took care of the problem once and for all.

> *By the multitude of thy merchandise they have filled the midst of thee with violence, and thou hast sinned: therefore I will cast thee as profane out of the mountain of God: and I will destroy thee, O covering cherub, from the midst of the stones of fire.*
>
> Ezekiel 28:16

Satan has been cast from the mountain of God. He might have access, but he no longer dwells there. He is no longer part of the heavenly establishment. He has been driven out of the sanctified position he previously occupied.

When the disciples rejoiced that they had authority over demons, Jesus said to them, "*I beheld Satan as lightning fall from heaven.*"[19] He affirmed that He had given them power over the enemy, but Jesus also told them,

"*Notwithstanding in this rejoice not, that the spirits are subject unto you; but rather rejoice, because your names are written in heaven.*" Satan is destined for everlasting judgment. We can celebrate because we have been freed from the same dreadful fate, and we get to spend eternity with our God.

How did sin enter Lucifer's heart? Where did it come from? It was birthed through his own self-worship. Like Narcissus, Lucifer looked at his own reflection, and he fell in love with himself.

*Thine heart was lifted up because of thy beauty, thou hast corrupted thy wisdom by reason of thy brightness: I will cast thee to the ground, I will lay thee before kings, that they may behold thee. Thou hast defiled thy sanctuaries by the multitude of thine iniquities, by the iniquity of thy traffick; therefore will I bring forth a fire from the midst of thee, it shall devour thee, and I will bring thee to ashes upon the earth in the sight of all them that behold thee.*

Ezekiel 28:17-18

His heart is filled with pride. God hates pride, because it is a conduit for sin to enter the premises. Satan has defiled his sanctuaries, which indicates that he was the one who ran the worship. As a result, God is going to cleanse the earth of him; remember, the earth is the stage where this drama will play out. John tells us in Revelation

20:9-10 that the great dragon Satan will lead a final rebellion at the end of time. It will fail; a fire will fall from heaven and consume them all, and Satan will be thrown into the lake of fire forever.

*All they that know thee among the people shall be astonished at thee: thou shalt be a terror, and never shalt thou be any more.*

Ezekiel 28:19

# Chapter 9
# The King of Babylon

We find a similar passage in Isaiah 14, in which God speaks through Isaiah to another world ruler - the King of Babylon. The prophet has to deal with the actual man sitting on the throne of Babylon, but the language pushes further, past the physical man to the power behind his throne.

We are used to wars between nations, and the 20th century was the bloodiest of them all. Yet, Paul reminds us of something exceedingly important in the final chapter of his letter to the Ephesians; our true battle is not against our fellow humans.

*For we wrestle not against flesh and blood, but against principalities, against powers, against the rulers of the darkness of this world, against spiritual wickedness in high places.*

Ephesians 6:12

What does that mean? It means that there are spiritual powers at work behind the scenes of our world. There are ranks of angels, and there are ranks of evil spirits - rulers of darkness and spiritual wickedness in high places.

In Isaiah 14, God is speaking to the King of Babylon, but more specifically to the spiritual wickedness in high places behind the power of the King of Babylon. The poetic language is hyperbolic when applied to the man on the physical throne, but very specific and literal when applied to the spiritual ruler at the back of the throne:

*How art thou fallen from heaven, O*
*Lucifer, son of the morning! how art thou*
*cut down to the ground, which didst*
*weaken the nations! For thou hast said*
*in thine heart, I will ascend into heaven,*
*I will exalt my throne above the stars of*
*God: I will sit also upon the mount of the*
*congregation, in the sides of the north: I*
*will ascend above the heights of the clouds;*
*I will be like the most High.*

Isaiah 14:12-14

### Lucifer

If we read this verse in Hebrew, the person being addressed is הילל בן־שחר *Heylel Shachar*, that is, "The Shining One, Son of the Morning." This is a description of the morning star, which is technically the planet we call Venus. When Jerome translated the Hebrew into Latin, he translated "The Shining One" into its Latin equivalent "Lucifer." It's noteworthy that the name *Heylel* comes from the root word *halal*, which means "praise." We recognize it in the word *Hallelujah*, which means, "Praise to Yahweh," with a sense of clapping in applause. This further gives us a sense that Lucifer's original job was to lead the worship in Heaven; his entire purpose was to bring God glory.

Instead, Lucifer chose to glorify himself. The Shining One desired to rise above all other beings, to sit on the mountain of congregations. He had the arrogance and the conceit to believe that he had what it took to be like God Himself. Ever since, he has sought to rob God and take the worship that belongs only to the Most High.

His rebellion was birthed in this self-worship, and it spread from him across the heavenly realms, until he managed to call a third of the angels into rebellion with him. Then the earth became formless and void. As we read in the events of Jeremiah 4:23-26, rebellion leads to chaos and destruction and confusion.

Now, he's fallen from heaven along with his legions of evil angelic cohorts. He became the tempter and the deceiver, and Paul warns us in 2 Corinthians 11:14, "*Satan himself is transformed into an angel of light.*" He remains the shining one, but he exchanged his form for that of the shining serpent in the garden. His original station was the highest and most glorious of the cherubim, full of beauty and wisdom and power. In his fallen state, he takes that glory and he twists it for evil, devastating purposes. He still hungers for power and the adoration that belongs to God alone. His sole purpose seems to be the deception and destruction of humankind. He seeks our worship and our utter ruin out of an enraged hatred for the Creator who loves us.

> *Be sober, be vigilant; because your adversary the devil, as a roaring lion, walketh about, seeking whom he may devour:*

1 Peter 5:8

> *Therefore rejoice, ye heavens, and ye that dwell in them. Woe to the inhabiters of the earth and of the sea! for the devil is come down unto you, having great wrath, because he knoweth that he hath but a short time.*

Revelation 12:12

God chose to let Satan go free, to deceive the nations as he chose. God allowed Satan to run the gamut and show us all how rebellion plays out. All of creation has experienced the pain and injury that rebellion causes. There's no secret about it now. Adam and Eve ate from the tree, and now we all know what evil is. We know the suffering it brings. In the end, we all have to make the decision about whom we are going to worship. Will we worship ourselves and our own egos, or will we worship the God of the universe? There can only be one ultimate will in the universe, and God will bring an end to Satan and all who follow after him.

We are all tainted by sin. We all deserve to be destroyed, but God also knew from the beginning that He would come to our rescue. He would sacrifice everything, and through the Messiah, He would bring all the broken pieces back together again.

> *Yet thou shalt be brought down to hell, to the sides of the pit. They that see thee shall narrowly look upon thee, and consider thee, saying, Is this the man that made the earth to tremble, that did shake kingdoms; That made the world as a wilderness, and destroyed the cities thereof; that opened not the house of his prisoners?*
>
> Isaiah 14:15-17

At the beginning of Revelation 20, we are told that the old serpent, the dragon Satan, will be bound and cast into the bottomless pit for a thousand years. It's interesting that a single angel with a chain is able to take hold of him and bind him. It's clear that Satan is not as all-powerful as he would like to think, no matter how much destruction he has caused. "*That made the earth to tremble... that made the world as a wilderness.*" That sounds a bit like Jeremiah 4:23-26 again.

Jesus calls Satan a murderer in John 8:44. He will not let his prisoners go willingly, yet Jesus tells us that the gates of Hell will fall before the Church.[20] We can tear down Satan's spiritual strongholds in the name of Christ. Still, God has allowed His enemies throughout history to kill His children. Jesus tells the Church at Smyrna in Revelation 2:10:

*Fear none of those things which thou shalt suffer: behold, the devil shall cast some of you into prison, that ye may be tried; and ye shall have tribulation ten days: be thou faithful unto death, and I will give thee a crown of life.*

There will be great persecution during the Tribulation as well. In Revelation 13:7 and Daniel 7:21, we find that Satan temporarily is able to defeat the saints physically. We learn that Satan's man of sin, the antichrist, will have the ability to make war against the faithful Jews and to physically prevail against them. It only lasts a short time, until Christ returns. He immediately takes over and gives the saints the kingdom. God merely has to give the word, and the dragon is bound and thrown into the pit. Here we find that God is talking to the antichrist as much as He is to Satan himself.

*All the kings of the nations, even all of them, lie in glory, every one in his own house. But thou art cast out of thy grave like an abominable branch, and as the raiment of those that are slain, thrust*

> *through with a sword, that go down to*
> *the stones of the pit; as a carcase trodden*
> *under feet. Thou shalt not be joined with*
> *them in burial, because thou hast destroyed*
> *thy land, and slain thy people: the seed of*
> *evildoers shall never be renowned.*

> Isaiah 14:18-20

This is very graphic. Great rulers tend to be buried in beautiful shrines that bring them ongoing honor. Not the antichrist. He will be like a carcass tossed out and trampled by crowds. Why? Because he has destroyed his land and slain his people. That's interesting. His land? His people?

> *The LORD of hosts hath sworn, saying,*
> *Surely as I have thought, so shall it come*
> *to pass; and as I have purposed, so shall it*
> *stand: That I will break the Assyrian in*
> *my land, and upon my mountains tread*
> *him under foot: then shall his yoke depart*
> *from off them, and his burden depart from*
> *off their shoulders.*

> Isaiah 14: 24-25

Wait. Notice that the antichrist is here called "the Assyrian." He is not a Russian European; he's an Assyrian. This is also what we find in Micah 5:5-6. The first world ruler Nimrod was an Assyrian. The final world dictator will be an Assyrian. Scripture makes that pretty clear, interestingly enough.

*This is the purpose that is purposed upon*
*the whole earth: and this is the hand that*
*is stretched out upon all the nations.*
*For the LORD of hosts hath purposed,*
*and who shall disannul it? and his hand is*
*stretched out, and who shall turn it back?*

Isaiah 14: 26-27

That's the origin of evil. It is the usurpation, the rebellion of the top angel who became Satan, our accuser, our tempter. The warfare is not between God and Satan, because that contest would last no time worth mentioning. Satan was successful at leading the first man to abort his allegiance to the God of the universe, but God has demonstrated His love and His power and His ability to rescue wayward man anyway. No matter how he strives, Satan is unsuccessful at winning the eternal worship he desires and in bringing humankind into ultimate subjection to himself.

Yet, each one of us currently lives on a battlefield, and the prize is the eternal salvation of each human being. We are at war, not against each other, but against those spiritual forces of wickedness that would drag us to hell with them if they could. Even though Christ's children are under His protection, we still face traps and snares, and we have loved ones still out there in the minefield.

# Chapter 10
# The Nature of Reality

What is reality? We think of reality as the physical world we touch and see and smell. It's the couch on which we sit and the floor on which we stand. When we trip and bang our shins, we feel physical pain, and we think *that's real.*

We need to reexamine what we think of as reality, because there is a world far more real than this one. We think of the spiritual as a fuzzy, imaginary place and the solid, physical world we can touch as the *actual* world. It's quite the opposite. This physical world will eventually burn up and disappear, but there is an eternal world that will last forever. That's the real world. This one… this world is just an illusion. It's a digital projection on a cosmic movie screen.

We need to have a better grasp of the spiritual world than whatever we get from television and movies. We tend to think of the spiritual in terms of common clichés that we can understand. We can't see it or feel it with our physical senses, so we imagine it in terms of clouds and other silly pictures that have nothing to do with anything. I think it will be useful for us to step back a little bit and get a different perspective of what we think of as reality.

## Our Empty World

There are people who do not believe in God because they do not believe in the spiritual realm. They can't conceive of its existence in any terms other than a fairy tale. If the spiritual realm does exist, where is it? This leads into the study of quantum physics, where we learn about subatomic particles, additional dimensions and hyperspaces.

Let's start by talking about the smallest thing you and I have the capacity to imagine: the atom. We all have seen sketches of atoms in school. We think of a simple hydrogen atom with a single positive proton in its nucleus and a single tiny negative electron spinning around it.

That hydrogen atom is incredibly small, but as small as it is, it is mostly empty space. There is a great deal of nothing between the proton nucleus and that one little orbiting electron. The hydrogen atom is about $1 \times 10^{-10}$ meters in diameter, while the nucleus alone is more than 100,000 times smaller at $1 \times 10^{-15}$ m. In other words, that single zippy electron increases the size of the atom by 100,000 times. If we used a golf ball to simulate our nucleus, the electron would be zooming around 1.3 miles away.

That 1.3 miles represents just the radius of the atom - a linear distance. If we want to calculate all the empty space involved in our atom with its golf-ball-sized proton nucleus, we'd have to cube that radius according to the formula $v = 4/3\ pr^3$. We recognize that the atom diameter is 100,000 times the diameter of the golf ball. The volume of the entire atom is (4/3) x 1000,000,000,000,000 times the size of that golf ball. A ratio of $1:10^{15}$ is difficult for us to appreciate. That's the same ratio as one second is to 31 million years. The volume of the hydrogen atom nucleus is a tiny, insignificant speck compared to the vast volume of the atom complete with electron.

We think the couch is real. We think the floor is real. We don't realize that most of what we think of as "reality" is actually just empty space. We struggle to appreciate just how little reality exists in the daily world in which we operate.

## Our Digital World

As we go into the field of the microcosm, we discover something even more shocking. We discover that everything is made up of indivisible units. This world we consider "real" is actually digital. Everything we know is made up of indivisible units - tiny building blocks that cannot be divided. Mass, energy, length - each has a limit. If I measure a line, I can divide it in half and measure again. I can do this over and over and over until my line becomes so small that I can no longer cut it in half. This length is called the Planck length, and it's much, much smaller than the diameter of an electron. It is a ridiculously minute length of $1.62 \times 10^{-35}$m - a length that is $10^{20}$m smaller than a proton. At the Planck length, any effort to make another division results in what is called "nonlocality." The line ceases to exist as an independent item. It suddenly becomes everywhere at once.

What does that mean? It means that our universe is digital, and it points to the understanding that we are living in what is ultimately a digital simulation.

Matter is not made of Planck-length pieces, but much larger units - still incomprehensibly small to us. Little packages called "quanta" are the particles that make up the fundamental parts of matter. Atoms are composed of protons, neutrons and electrons, and protons and neutrons are made up of even smaller tiny pieces called quarks, leptons and gluons.

## Quantum Entanglement

Quanta like electrons, photons and protons behave in bizarre, confusing ways. They behave in ways that don't make sense to us. We think that particles should behave like billiard balls. We can calculate how billiard balls will move if they are hit from a certain direction with a certain amount of force. Subatomic particles aren't like that. They don't behave themselves at all, and physicists have to make conclusions on quantum behavior based on statistics - probabilities - rather than on observations of any single particle.

What is especially troubling about quanta is that we can change how they behave just by looking at them. What? Yes. Just by observing them, we affect what they do. This means that we have a hard time saying for certain what particles are doing when we are *not* looking at them.[21]

What is even more disturbing is that every photon in the universe seems to know what every other photon is doing - instantly. In 1982, Alain Aspect, Jean Dalibard, and Gérard Roger at the Institute of Theoretical and Applied Optics in Paris directly demonstrated that two separated particles were able to communicate faster than the speed of light.[22]

## Hyperspaces

One of the great breakthroughs Einstein made was describing space in four dimensions rather than three. He recognized that time itself is a dimension, and physicists since have concluded there must be additional spatial dimensions beyond the ones we can directly see and feel.

Angels are not ethereal, fairy tale beings. They are sentient, knowledgeable individuals who exist in what I call the "metacosm" - those dimensions that are beyond our direct reach. Angels can enter our four-dimensional time-space domain, but they are not constrained by it like we are. They are able to travel into our environment, but they can remove themselves from our eyesight back into the larger domain that is native to them.

The 20th century gave us many advances in quantum physics, and theoretical physicists began to realize that the math worked better when we added additional dimensions to the four that Einstein described. In 1921,

Theodor Kaluza argued for a fifth dimension, and in 1926 Oskar Kline took Kaluza's ideas and added some quantum trimming to the idea. The resulting Kaluza-Kline theory of gravitation and electromagnetism used five dimensions to explain our universe. In 1953, famous physicist Wolfgang Pauli extended Kaluza and Klein's five dimensions to six, fitting Einstein's field equations of general relativity into a six-dimensional format. A few years later, Yang and Mills used six dimensions to reconcile electromagnetics for both the weak and strong nuclear forces. By simply adding dimensions, these imponderable things suddenly yielded understanding and clarity.

Then came the parade of string theories during the 1980s. In 1981, theorist Edward Witten showed that 11 was the smallest number of dimensions that was big enough to contain the gauge groups of the Standard Model. Later at the 1995 string theory conference at the University of Southern California, Witten presented his now famous M-Theory in which he unified the five popular string theories. The M is said to stand for Magic or Mystery or Matrix Theory, and it predicts at least 10 dimensions (3+1+6). There are the three dimensions of space and one dimension of time that we currently experience, plus six additional dimensions – each wound up as one-dimensional vibrating superstrings. Throw in supergravity and superstring theorists suggest a total of 11 dimensions.

These additional dimensions offer an explanation for the "where" of the spiritual realm. A unified Theory of Everything has so far eluded theoretical physicists, but even while the mathematicians work out their equations, I believe angels watch them unseen from these hyperspaces.

Ephesians 3 offers us an interesting verse that hints at these matters. Paul talks about the love of Christ, and he refers to four spatial dimensions rather than three:

> *That Christ may dwell in your hearts by faith; that ye, being rooted and grounded in love, May be able to comprehend with all saints what is the breadth, and length, and depth, and height; And to know the love of Christ, which passeth knowledge, that ye might be filled with all the fulness of God.*

> Ephesians 3:17-19

Paul wants his readers to comprehend the breadth, the length, the depth and the height. He lists four dimensions. These words in the Greek are:

πλάτος - *platos* - breadth
μῆκος - *mekos* - length
βάθος - *bathos* - deep or depths
ὕψος - *hupsos* - height or heavenly

We can argue that all additional dimensions are included in that fourth term, in the broadness of the heights of heaven. We can see the breadth, length and depth of things, but all others are in the spiritual realms. The word *hupsos* has its root in the word ὑπέρ - *huper* - from which we get our word "hyper," so it's appropriate that these additional dimensions are called "hyperspaces."

What is really real?

We only directly experience the tip of the iceberg.

# Chapter 11
# Peeking Behind the Curtain

There is a hidden world all around us, beyond our sight. Most of the time, we are unaware of the spiritual activity taking place right next to us. We are blind to the spiritual battles being waged on our behalf.

Remember Ephesians 6:12:

*For we wrestle not against flesh and blood, but against principalities, against powers, against the rulers of the darkness of this world, against spiritual wickedness in high places.*

Ephesians 6:12

That's scary stuff. There are ranks of fallen angels and demons at work in this broken world. It's especially scary, because we cannot see our enemy with our physical eyes. We can't hear him with our physical ears. If a group of thugs approach us in a dark alley, at least we know they're there. We can see the knives in their hands. We have a clue about the trouble that faces us. Not so spiritually. We have no clue what evil powers lurk around us.

Maybe that's a good thing. Maybe that's a mercy. Maybe we don't want to know.

At the same time, we also can't see the armies of angels that God has placed around us for our protection. God's angels outnumber Satan's 2-to-1. We have authority over the spiritual forces of wickedness, because Jesus Christ has given us that authority. We don't have to fear the evil, because we can defeat Satan's forces by prayer and the power of God working in us.

I take the view that fallen angels and demons are not the same thing. Fallen angels are vastly more powerful than demons. Angels can materialize and become visible to our physical eyes, while demons are constantly searching for a body to inhabit.[23] Angels can engage in physical combat and other physical activity. In Isaiah 37:36, the Angel of the LORD slew 185,000 Assyrians in one night. Demons are powerless except to the extent that they can influence, guide and possess a person. Demons seem to be desperate for embodiment.[24]

Occasionally, however, the Bible does allow us a view from the backstage out into the greater audience of the spiritual realm.

## Outnumbered in Dothan

For example, Elisha gives us a marvelous bit of perspective in 2 Kings 6. Here we find that the Syrian leader Ben Hadad is making regular attacks on its southern neighbor Israel. However, the prophet Elisha consistently warns the king of Israel of Syrian ambushes, and the Israelis escape time and time again. After being thwarted repeatedly, Ben Hadad demands to know who among his own servants is betraying him and giving secrets to the Israelis:

> *Therefore the heart of the king of Syria was sore troubled for this thing; and he called his servants, and said unto them, Will ye not shew me which of us is for the king of Israel? And one of his servants said, None, my lord, O king: but Elisha, the prophet that is in Israel, telleth the king of Israel the words that thou speakest in thy bedchamber.*

2 Kings 6:11-12

Elisha has a spiritual wiretap on Ben Hadad; God tells him even the things whispered in Ben Hadad's bedroom. God has no problem invading the Syrian king's privacy, and the king wants to put a stop to it. He finds out where Elisha is living, and he sends horses and chariots and bazookas[25] and "a great host" down to Dothan to go collect Elisha and bring him back to Syria for a chat.

> *And when the servant of the man of God was risen early, and gone forth, behold, an host compassed the city both with horses and chariots. And his servant said unto him, Alas, my master! how shall we do?*

2 Kings 6:15

Elisha's servant wakes up in the morning, sees the Syrian army surrounding them, and panics. Of course he does. Any one of us would have panicked too. It's just two guys against a great Syrian host, and the servant knows that his master has been spiritually spying on the Syrians for the king of Israel. The servant assumes that they're dead meat.

Elisha looks at the situation with a different set of eyes. He has the ability to see past the physical mask of this world into the full reality beyond.

> *And he answered, Fear not: for they that*
> *be with us are more than they that be*
> *with them. And Elisha prayed, and said,*
> *LORD, I pray thee, open his eyes, that he*
> *may see. And the LORD opened the eyes of*
> *the young man; and he saw: and, behold,*
> *the mountain was full of horses and*
> *chariots of fire round about Elisha.*
>
> 2 Kings 6:16-17

Elisha's servant can hear them revving their engines out there, and he's scared. Elisha's reassurance is not a glib cliché, however. "Don't be afraid. There are more on our side than on theirs." That statement is based on Elisha's full understanding of their true situation, and he's being very patient here, because his servant should have more faith by now. Elisha prays and asks God to open the servant's eyes and make him able to see the spiritual world as well. What does the servant see? The fiery horses and chariots of the Lord around the Syrians, covering the mountain.

Does Elisha hide? No. In boldness, he approaches the Syrians and says, "Hey! You're in the wrong place." They are given a temporary blindness (whether in their ability to reason or in their actual physical sight) and they follow Elisha right into the capital city of Samaria. There the king of Israel could have easily slain them all, but Elisha tells him to feed the bewildered soldiers and send them home.

> *And it came to pass, when they were come into Samaria, that Elisha said, LORD, open the eyes of these men, that they may see. And the LORD opened their eyes, and they saw; and, behold, they were in the midst of Samaria. And the king of Israel said unto Elisha, when he saw them, My father, shall I smite them? shall I smite them? And he answered, Thou shalt not smite them: wouldest thou smite those whom thou hast taken captive with thy sword and with thy bow? set bread and water before them, that they may eat and drink, and go to their master.*

2 Kings 6:20-22

## Spiritual Guardians

> *A thousand shall fall at thy side, and ten thousand at thy right hand; but it shall*

*not come nigh thee. Only with thine eyes
shalt thou behold and see the reward of
the wicked. Because thou hast made the
LORD, which is my refuge, even the most
High, thy habitation; There shall no evil
befall thee, neither shall any plague come
nigh thy dwelling. For he shall give his
angels charge over thee, to keep thee in all
thy ways. They shall bear thee up in their
hands, lest thou dash thy foot against
a stone.*

Psalm 91:7-12

This is the very passage that Satan quoted to Jesus on the top of the Temple, twisting the words into a meaning they did not have. Satan tempted Jesus to put God to the test by jumping off the top of the Temple. That's just foolish. It's a reckless presumption to test God to prove His power.

Satan certainly sought to twist this passage, however, for the very fact of its power and significance. The psalmist encourages us to have confidence in God's protection and provision as we go through this dangerous world. When we are walking in God's will, there is nothing that can touch us without His say so. He is our hiding place. He is our defender, and when God is on our side, we can walk in safety and confidence even through the darkest places.

Most of us have little understanding of the angelic protection surrounding us every day. We pray, "Lord, please place your angels around us," but we don't always appreciate that He hears our prayers and *does* so. We are not left defenseless, and nothing is too difficult for God. If we only look at this world with physical eyes, we can live in fear and desperation, unaware of the great power and provision and protection available to us. When we look at things through spiritual eyes, however, we can have peace and confidence even in the scariest situations. The Bible is full of reminders that physical difficulties are just an illusion in light of God's power working in our lives.

> *Some trust in chariots, and some in horses:*
> *but we will remember the name of the*
> *LORD our God. They are brought down*
> *and fallen: but we are risen, and stand*
> *upright.*

Psalm 20:7-8

> *Yea, though I walk through the valley of*
> *the shadow of death, I will fear no evil:*
> *for thou art with me; thy rod and thy staff*
> *they comfort me.*

Psalm 23:4

> *No weapon that is formed against thee*
> *shall prosper; and every tongue that*
> *shall rise against thee in judgment thou*
> *shalt condemn. This is the heritage of*
> *the servants of the LORD, and their*
> *righteousness is of me, saith the LORD.*

Isaiah 54:17

If that really soaks into our minds and hearts, how much freedom and joy we will experience! We can know we are not alone as we go to work and school. As we struggle to pay our bills, as we deal with our neighbors, our bosses, our families and the many troubles of this world, we can have great peace knowing that God is taking care of things as we place ourselves in His care.

There's an evil element in the spiritual world. As I mentioned earlier, Satan's legions are outnumbered by God's 2 to 1, but they can still cause trouble. We're going to get a glimpse of this - what I like to call The Dark Side.

# Chapter 12
# The Dark Side

In his famous books *This Present Darkness* (1986) and *Piercing the Darkness* (1988), author Frank Peretti made a bold effort to portray the spiritual warfare that goes on behind the scenes of our world. There's a great deal of his imagination at work in the books, but they make us start thinking about the sorts of battles that might very well take place in the heavenlies - even along the leaf-strewn streets of small-town America.

The Scriptures do tell us that there are spiritual rulers over the nations of the world. I'm confident that Iran and Iraq, Brazil and Russia, England and Serbia and China each have principalities and powers, ranks of spiritual beings, at the backs of the humans who sit in the seats of government. In Daniel 10 we learn about three of these: the wicked princes of Persia and Greece as adversaries, and the protector of Israel, Michael the archangel himself.

> *In the third year of Cyrus king of Persia a thing was revealed unto Daniel, whose name was called Belteshazzar; and the thing was true, but the time appointed was long: and he understood the thing,*

*and had understanding of the vision. In
those days I Daniel was mourning three
full weeks. I ate no pleasant bread, neither
came flesh nor wine in my mouth, neither
did I anoint myself at all, till three whole
weeks were fulfilled.*

Daniel 10:1-3

This is the third year of Cyrus the Great, and
Daniel has retired. Cyrus has already allowed the
Jews to return to their land, according to Ezra 1.
It's been several years since Ezekiel's prophetic
ministry, although Ezekiel and Daniel were
roughly contemporaneous. Daniel is now quite
an old man. He remains in Babylon where he has
spent the majority of his life, but his heart still
bleeds for the people and land of Israel.

The Jewish exiles that returned from Babylon
have begun to rebuild the Temple in Jerusalem.
Fewer than 50,000 actually took advantage of
Cyrus' decree to return under Ezra and later
Nehemiah, but the work of rebuilding Israel has
started. Something weighs on Daniel, though,
and he goes into a time of mourning for three full
weeks. He's not worried about his appearance or
what food he eats with this great weight on his
heart. That's a serious fast, especially for a man as
old as Daniel now is.

*And in the four and twentieth day of the
first month, as I was by the side of the great
river, which is Hiddekel; Then I lifted*

*up mine eyes, and looked, and behold a
certain man clothed in linen, whose loins
were girded with fine gold of Uphaz: His
body also was like the beryl, and his face as
the appearance of lightning, and his eyes as
lamps of fire, and his arms and his feet like
in colour to polished brass, and the voice of
his words like the voice of a multitude.*

Daniel 10:4-6

We do not learn the name of this angel, but
we know he's not Gabriel, because Daniel already
knew Gabriel from Chapter 8. This new visitor
is glorious and commanding, and we soon learn
of his great power as a as a warrior. Still, he does
not worry Daniel with his name. Some scholars
believe this man is the Lord Jesus Christ, but Jesus
would not have needed the help of Michael –
as this angel does. I believe Daniel is being met
by a senior angel, whose very presence takes away
all of Daniel's strength.

*And I Daniel alone saw the vision: for the
men that were with me saw not the vision;
but a great quaking fell upon them, so that
they fled to hide themselves. Therefore I
was left alone, and saw this great vision,
and there remained no strength in me:
for my comeliness was turned in me into
corruption, and I retained no strength.
Yet heard I the voice of his words: and
when I heard the voice of his words,*

*then was I in a deep sleep on my face, and
my face toward the ground. And, behold,
an hand touched me, which set me upon
my knees and upon the palms of my hands.*

Daniel 10:7-10

Throughout the scriptures, we find that awe,
humility and physical weakness always seem to
accompany confrontations between humans and
these angelic beings. They are nothing to laugh
about. Each time they show up, they cause men to
fall to the ground, helplessly weak and trembling,
by the sheer glory of their presence.

*And he said unto me, O Daniel, a man
greatly beloved, understand the words that
I speak unto thee, and stand upright: for
unto thee am I now sent. And when he
had spoken this word unto me, I stood
trembling. Then said he unto me, Fear not,
Daniel: for from the first day that thou
didst set thine heart to understand, and to
chasten thyself before thy God, thy words
were heard, and I am come for thy words.*

Daniel 10:11-12

Daniel has been fasting and praying for three
weeks. Three weeks. The angel tells Daniel that
God heard him as soon as he started praying. God
sent the angel immediately in response to Daniel's
prayer - he was sent specifically to communicate
to Daniel - but it took three entire weeks for

this powerful and majestic being to arrive at his destination. Why? We find out the messenger ran into some roadblocks on his way to Daniel. As he traveled, another spiritual power came against him and prevented his passage.

> *But the prince of the kingdom of Persia withstood me one and twenty days: but, lo, Michael, one of the chief princes, came to help me; and I remained there with the kings of Persia. Now I am come to make thee understand what shall befall thy people in the latter days: for yet the vision is for many days.*

Daniel 10:13-14

The "prince of the kingdom of Persia" is clearly not the human ruler of the day. The angel is referring to some creature, some evil spiritual power behind the human kingdom. This supernatural opposition did not want the angel to deliver his message, which tells us the message has great importance. We assume that the angel would normally be able to fly straight from God's throne to Daniel, but this mighty thing got in his way. The enemy prince of Persia was no small enemy. The angel spent those three full weeks battling past him, and he didn't have success until Michael arrived to help him. Again, that is why I don't think the angel is an incarnation of Christ. Christ would not have needed Michael's help.

Here we learn that Michael is one of the chief princes. Of all angelic powers, he's up at the top. He's a military guy, and he's the one that confronted Satan over the body of Moses.[26] I believe the voice of the archangel at Christ's return is Michael's voice.[27]

On a side note, Michael's contention with Satan over Moses' body is a mystery. God buried Moses personally, according to Deuteronomy 34:6-7, yet Michael had to fight Satan over his body. Dead bodies rot away and turn to dust. What's the issue? We will have new bodies when we are resurrected.

Apparently, Moses' body was important in some way. We know he shows up at the Transfiguration in Matthew 17. Moses and Elijah appear and talk to Jesus. I also believe that Moses and Elijah are the witnesses in Revelation 11. Both Moses and Elijah have a special role yet to play during the end times.

There is another issue here that's quite important. What would have happened if Daniel had stopped fasting after the 19th day? What if he gave up on praying before the angel arrived? We don't know. We presume that the 21 days of fasting were necessary as the angel spent those three weeks fighting past the resistance. It's a good question.

*And when he had spoken such words unto me, I set my face toward the ground, and I became dumb. And, behold, one like the similitude of the sons of men touched my lips: then I opened my mouth, and spake, and said unto him that stood before me, O my lord, by the vision my sorrows are turned upon me, and I have retained no strength. For how can the servant of this my lord talk with this my lord? for as for me, straightway there remained no strength in me, neither is there breath left in me. Then there came again and touched me one like the appearance of a man, and he strengthened me, And said, O man greatly beloved, fear not: peace be unto thee, be strong, yea, be strong. And when he had spoken unto me, I was strengthened, and said, Let my lord speak; for thou hast strengthened me. Then said he, Knowest thou wherefore I come unto thee? and now will I return to fight with the prince of Persia: and when I am gone forth, lo, the prince of Grecia shall come. But I will shew thee that which is noted in the scripture of truth: and there is none that holdeth with me in these things, but Michael your prince.*

Daniel 10:15-21

After this, the angel proceeds to give Daniel the vision described in chapters 11 and 12 - an amazing prophecy about the future. It describes in advance the reigns of Alexander the Great and his four generals, but it also lays out events that will take place at the end of time.

A full 400 years pass between the books of Malachi and Matthew, and people often call these the "silent years." It's not true, though. We find events in those years detailed here at the end of Daniel. From Alexander to Cleopatra to Antiochus IV, God tells Daniel what is going to happen, and the descriptions are so accurate, historians have argued they were written after the fact.

The angel tells Daniel that when he leaves again, he'll have to return to fight against the supernatural prince of Persia first, and then the supernatural prince of Greece. Pay attention to something, though. Who is the prince of Israel? Michael. Not all the spiritual heads of the countries are evil beings. Michael is the righteous warrior archangel of God who serves to protect Israel. That makes us wonder which spiritual forces are at work over the leadership of America. We have called America, "One Nation Under God" and our money boldly states, "In God We Trust." Are those words true? Who is the spiritual head of America, and does that supernatural leadership change as readily as we do?

The angel left Daniel to go fight the prince of Persia and then the prince of Greece. Angels clearly do not experience time the same way we do; the Greek Empire didn't follow the Persian Empire until 200 years later.

This glorious angelic being gives us a glimpse behind the scenes of our visible world. From his brief explanation, "Sorry, the traffic was terrible," we learn that angelic adversaries fight over world governments. There is a war going on that we don't get to see with our flesh and blood eyes. Daniel 10 teaches us something else; our prayers matter. James tells us, *"The effectual fervent prayer of a righteous man availeth much."*[28] When we humble ourselves before the Almighty God, He hears us and acts on our behalf. We have both an impact and a responsibility in this heavenly warfare, and if we who are called by the name of Christ appreciate this fact, we can have great spiritual influence on our own families and communities and countries.

Satan is our accuser and our enemy. He is the tempter. He is a liar and a murderer. We know that he was created a glorious being by God, but he corrupted himself by his pride and self-worship. God allowed Satan to proceed with his rebellion and lead others with him, but there will come a day when his reign of terror is ended.

# Chapter 13
# The Red Dragon

Ezekiel 28 tells us that Satan was cast down from God's government in heaven, but he is still allowed access to stand and accuse us. In Job 1 and Zechariah 3, we find Satan in heaven to criticize God's people. His goal, however, has always been to thwart the plan of God.

In Revelation 12, John describes a woman and a man child in heaven, and the red dragon with seven heads and ten horns waits to eat the woman's child at his birth:

*And there appeared a great wonder in heaven; a woman clothed with the sun, and the moon under her feet, and upon her head a crown of twelve stars: And she being with child cried, travailing in birth, and pained to be delivered. And there appeared another wonder in heaven; and behold a great red dragon, having seven heads and ten horns, and seven crowns upon his heads. And his tail drew the third part of the stars of heaven, and did cast them to the earth: and the dragon stood*

*before the woman which was ready to be*
*delivered, for to devour her child as soon as*
*it was born. And she brought forth a man*
*child, who was to rule all nations with a*
*rod of iron: and her child was caught up*
*unto God, and to his throne.*

Revelation 12:1-5

This woman clothed with the sun is easily identified as Israel by her crown of 12 stars. After Joseph tells his dream in Genesis 37:9, his father Jacob immediately interprets it in the next verse. The sun and moon are identified by Jacob as himself and his wife, and the 12 stars are his 12 sons. We know the woman in Revelation 12 is not the Church, because the Church is the *virgin* bride of Christ. This woman is Israel giving birth to a man child. We recognize him as the Messiah because he is to rule with a rod of iron.[29] Satan as the red dragon intends to consume the man child when he is born, but the boy is caught up to the throne of God.

*And the woman fled into the wilderness,*
*where she hath a place prepared of God,*
*that they should feed her there a thousand*
*two hundred and threescore days. And*
*there was war in heaven: Michael and*
*his angels fought against the dragon; and*
*the dragon fought and his angels, And*
*prevailed not; neither was their place*
*found any more in heaven. And the great*

*dragon was cast out, that old serpent,
called the Devil, and Satan, which
deceiveth the whole world: he was cast out
into the earth, and his angels were cast out
with him.*

Revelation 12:6-9

The woman escapes into the wilderness where she'll be cared for three and a half years. Michael and his angels go to battle and conquer the dragon and his angels, and the losers are thrown down to the earth. In his rage, the dragon goes off to persecute the woman for those 1,260 days. We know that this is a literal period of time, because it is described in every which way - 1260 days, 42 months and three and a half years[30] - all based on the original 360-day year. This is the Great Tribulation - the last half of a seven-year period.

The man child is the seed of the woman. He's a human like us, born of Israel, but caught up to heaven to the throne of God for a time. This might also be a picture of the Rapture, since we are all the body of Christ. He's our Kinsman Redeemer, the Messiah, and He's going to rule all the nations with the rod of iron.

The "rod of iron" idiom is used in both the Old and New Testaments to describe His rule.[31] When we get sick of the corruption and crime rampant in our world today, we can be glad there will be a righteous ruler who will nip all of that in the bud. Isaiah 11 tells us that His just reign will be a time of great peace.

Before that time, however, Satan will take his vengeance out on the earth in an attempt to destroy the woman:

> *And I heard a loud voice saying in heaven,*
> *Now is come salvation, and strength, and*
> *the kingdom of our God, and the power of*
> *his Christ: for the accuser of our brethren is*
> *cast down, which accused them before our*
> *God day and night. And they overcame*
> *him by the blood of the Lamb, and by the*
> *word of their testimony; and they loved not*
> *their lives unto the death. Therefore rejoice,*
> *ye heavens, and ye that dwell in them.*
> *Woe to the inhabiters of the earth and*
> *of the sea! for the devil is come down*
> *unto you, having great wrath, because he*
> *knoweth that he hath but a short time.*
> *And when the dragon saw that he was cast*
> *unto the earth, he persecuted the woman*
> *which brought forth the man child.*
>
> Revelation 12:10-13

God expelled Satan from heaven, from the mountain of God's government, back in Ezekiel 28. Yet, he was still able to access God's throne as our accuser. During the tribulation, however, Satan will be thrown out of heaven permanently and restricted to the earth. This will be an intense time. Satan knows the Scriptures, and he knows he has a short window of opportunity. When that time comes, Satan will have to move fast to produce as much destruction as he can. After 42 months, Christ returns to take up His kingdom as the heir of King David. Satan will be chained up and imprisoned in the abyss for 1000 years, and human beings will have no excuse for any rebellion, other than that which rises up in their own hearts. Satan will be bound, unable to tempt or deceive the nations.

> *And I saw an angel come down from heaven, having the key of the bottomless pit and a great chain in his hand. And he laid hold on the dragon, that old serpent, which is the Devil, and Satan, and bound him a thousand years, And cast him into the bottomless pit, and shut him up, and set a seal upon him, that he should deceive the nations no more, till the thousand years should be fulfilled: and after that he must be loosed a little season.*

Revelation 20:1-3

After a brief release at the end of millennium, the dragon leads a great army of rebels against Jerusalem, but it's a short fight. Fire falls from heaven and consumes them all. Then Satan meets his end. He is cast in the lake of fire forever.

> *And they went up on the breadth of the earth, and compassed the camp of the*

*saints about, and the beloved city: and*
*fire came down from God out of heaven,*
*and devoured them. And the devil that*
*deceived them was cast into the lake of fire*
*and brimstone, where the beast and the*
*false prophet are, and shall be tormented*
*day and night for ever and ever.*

Revelation 20:9-10

And that's that for the great dragon, called Satan and the Devil. His destiny is sealed. What's more, he knows it. He may continue in a form of self-delusion, however, because ever since the gap between verses 1 and 2 of Genesis, Satan has done his utmost to upset God's plan.

## Thwarting Satan

From the beginning of Creation, Satan has tried his best to destroy the humans whom God loves. We see an ongoing pattern. Satan attempts to interrupt God's purposes, and time and again God thwarts Satan's efforts and protects His plan of salvation.

Satan succeeded in corrupting Adam. When God revealed His plan that both heaven and earth would be redeemed by a man from the line of Adam, Satan made his attack on Adam's line. In Genesis 6, we find fallen angels start producing children with human women, infecting the human gene pool. This led to the Flood, in which only Noah and his family survived. Not only was Noah a righteous man who feared

God, but he was "perfect in his generations."[32] His line was not mingled with input by the fallen angels.

As God continued to reveal His plan, it became clear that the blessing of redemption would go through the line of Abraham. At that point, Abraham's seed became the primary target of Satan in Genesis 12 and 20, when Abraham almost allows his wife to be taken by another man. Satan then sought to destroy Abraham's descendants through the line of Jacob. In Genesis 50, the children of Israel went down into Egypt to escape famine, but they were soon oppressed and forced into slavery.

In Exodus 1 we find that Pharaoh commanded the systematic slaughter of all male Hebrew babies. Again, God came to the rescue, and later, Moses was used by God to miraculously strike Egypt with plagues. God instituted the Passover, a foreshadowing of Christ's sacrifice, and Moses led the Israelites out of Egypt following God's directions. Pharaoh pursued, but he and his armies were thrown into the sea.

God had promised Abraham that in 400 years his children would come back to the land of Canaan as a great nation.[33] His plan was revealed, and Satan began laying down minefields in the form of Nephilim in the Promised Land. As a result, God commanded Joshua to wipe out every man, woman and child in Canaan. The Israelites weren't to harm the women and children of the surrounding nations that weren't infected - just the Canaanites.[34]

God revealed His plans for the line of David in 2 Samuel 7, and Satan proceeded to make efforts to kill off that line. David's descendant Jehoram killed all his brothers in 2 Chronicles 21:4. His son Ahaziah became king after him, but when Ahaziah died, his mother Athaliah attempted to kill all his sons and take the throne for herself. In 2 Chronicles 22:11, however, Ahaziah's sister rescued his young son Joash and hid him in the Temple for six years, protecting the line of David.

In the book of Esther, Haman attempted to have all the Jews in the Persian Empire slaughtered, but his plans are dumped on top of him by God's insiders Esther and Mordecai. After Jesus was born, Herod attempted to kill every child in Bethlehem two-years-old and younger, but God warned Joseph in a dream to take Mary and the child and flee to Egypt.[35]

Jesus grew into a man and began His ministry, but the efforts to obstruct God's plan continued relentlessly. Satan tried to tempt Jesus to sin, but that didn't work. Then, when Jesus announced His ministry in Luke 4:18, the people in the synagogue were enraged by the things He said and attempted to throw Him over a cliff. He just walked through them to safety.[36] When a great storm at sea threatened to swamp the boat He was in, Jesus just stood and rebuked it.[37] I don't think the storms Jesus lived through were natural storms. The experienced fishermen were terrified for their lives during the storms, and I believe they were supernatural in their origin. This is why Jesus rebuked the wind.

Time and again Satan has attempted to wipe out the line of the Messiah and to thwart God's plan. Time and again, God has taken care of the situation. Each time God reveals His plan, Satan focuses his energies on obstructing it. However, God's purposes are ultimately accomplished, regardless.

In the end, Jesus was killed. The Messiah of the world was murdered on a Roman cross. It appeared to all that the enemy had won. The King was dead. Yet, it was all part of God's entire plan of redemption, written out many centuries in advance. Jesus fulfilled the sacrificial system of the Law. He became the Passover Lamb whose blood protects us from death. He became the scape goat on Yom Kippur. He became our High Priest, able to enter the Holy of Holies to present the sacrifice and sprinkle the blood to cover our sins. He rose again, and He will never die, making Him an everlasting High Priest who will never need a replacement.

Revelation 12 tells us that Satan isn't finished, even now. He's been conquered, but he intends to do as much damage as he can before his inevitable end. He is still striking out at God's people, and God continues to promote His plan just the same. Satan will make his grand move during a seven-year period through his false messiah, through whom he'll work to deceive the entire world. During the last 42 months of that period, he will severely persecute the people of Israel, the people of the true Messiah.

The dragon is still at it. We need to understand his agenda and his resources, because he's not through. You and I are the pawns and the price in this drama. Remember Satan's titles. He's the prince of this world. He's the prince of the power of the air. He's the god of this age and the ruler of darkness.

## America on the Rocks

America is in moral free fall. We are not victims of the immoral agendas of certain political groups. No. We're victims of spiritual warfare. The world media are adept at masking truth. They go out of their way to hide the truth and spin news to promote an anti-God agenda. We have courts without justice and corruption runs rampant. What used to be patriotism is now replaced by anger. Our schools have deteriorated and our youth are deliberately dumbed down. We've replaced our traditional heritage with multiculturalism, revisionism and values relativism.

It used to be that even the simplest peasants in America believed that sending their kids to college meant they would at least learn right from wrong. It's ironic that our colleges now deny the existence of right and wrong. Governments have always loved crises. They provide the rationale for increased budgets and bureaucracies and subjugation of the population. What creates social crisis? Immorality. Large numbers of people in our government are actively promoting every kind of immorality in the name of liberty, and the result is more people in both physical and spiritual bondage. The mobs love to be fed and clothed, all the while being given the license to make whatever foolish decisions they want. That's one of the many reasons that our founding fathers avoided making us a democracy. A democracy is mob rule. We were set up as a republic, which has democratic features with safeguards like the separation of powers and due process of law.

We call ourselves One Nation Under God. Are we? It says, "In God We Trust" on our money. That is true for a large number of Americans, but the percentage that reject the rule of God and God's Word appears to be growing day by day.

# Chapter 14
# Our Heavy Artillery

We are in a spiritual war, and more than just our physical lives are at stake. Every day people make decisions that have eternal consequences. We know that we are more than conquerors through Christ who loves us.[38] As we take part in this ongoing battle for the hearts and spirits of humankind, we absolutely need to be prepared. God has not left us defenseless. We have spiritual guardians, angels ready to hold us up.[39] We have also been issued a set of armor, able to help us withstand the enemy.

> *Finally, my brethren, be strong in the*
> *Lord, and in the power of his might.*
> *Put on the whole armour of God, that ye*
> *may be able to stand against the wiles of*
> *the devil.*

Ephesians 6:10-11

Notice, Paul tells us to put on the power of the Lord's might. We often think that it's our job to be the strong ones, but we usually fail. We need His strength and His might. We need to put on His armor so we can stand against the tricky enemy of our souls.

## The Armor of God

*For we wrestle not against flesh and blood,*
*but against principalities, against powers,*
*against the rulers of the darkness of this*
*world, against spiritual wickedness in high*
*places. Wherefore take unto you the whole*
*armour of God, that ye may be able to*
*withstand in the evil day, and having done*
*all, to stand.*

Ephesian 6:12-13

Here's our threat assessment right here.
There are evil spiritual forces at work in places of
power, and they are our true enemies. The people
around us are not our adversaries; they are humans
for whom Christ died. Each of us is precious to
God, and only God knows who ultimately belongs
to Him. We are not out to destroy even the most
aggravating, foul person with terrible behavior.
We are out to take down the strongholds of the
enemy of all souls.

Again, Paul tells us to put on the armor of
God, and to stand steadfastly.

*Stand therefore, having your loins girt*
*about with truth, and having on the*
*breastplate of righteousness; And your feet*
*shod with the preparation of the gospel of*
*peace; Above all, taking the shield of faith,*
*wherewith ye shall be able to quench all*
*the fiery darts of the wicked. And take the*

*helmet of salvation, and the sword of the*
*Spirit, which is the word of God:*

Ephesians 6:14-17

The first item Paul lists is the Belt of Truth. In a culture where people wore robes, it was difficult to run and fight with one's robe trailing down around one's ankles. They pulled their robes through their legs and tucked them into their belts, enabling them to run - to run and not trip and fall. Truth is the first thing. We need to have the truth firmly wrapped around us.

Next, Paul tells us to put on the breastplate of righteousness. That's God's righteousness, not our own. This is His armor He's giving to us.

Many people have assumed that Paul is taking these idioms from the Praetorian Guard who was chained to him in prison. In fact, he takes armor descriptions from Isaiah, and he builds on them.

*And he saw that there was no man, and*
*wondered that there was no intercessor:*
*therefore his arm brought salvation unto*
*him; and his righteousness, it sustained*
*him. For he put on righteousness as a*
*breastplate, and an helmet of salvation*
*upon his head; and he put on the garments*
*of vengeance for clothing, and was clad*
*with zeal as a cloke.*

Isaiah 59:16-17

The breastplate of righteousness is critical, because it protects the core of our being. Those are the kinds of attacks that are life threatening. A hit in the arm or shoulder can do damage, but we can survive them. God's breastplate of righteousness protects us from deadly wounds. We need to have security in the righteousness that comes through Christ alone. We need that protection, or the enemy will drop us.

We must have our feet shod with the preparation of the gospel of peace. Anybody who has trained in hand-to-hand combat knows the importance of footwork. At the Naval Academy, we were required to take a year of boxing and a year of wrestling as part of the program. I discovered that I just hate boxing. I happen to have kind of a long reach, so I didn't get clobbered too badly, but I did learn the necessity of proper footwork. If we're going to be in battle, we need to be prepared and well trained.

The Romans understood the value of a good shield. The word Paul uses here is θυρεος *thureos* - a large door-like shield that could protect the entire body. The Roman legionnaires used their shields together as a single unit, overlapping and sometimes forming the shape of a turtle shell. This cooperative effort protected them from missiles and items thrown from walls, and they knew the importance of leaving no holes exposed.

Are there holes in our shields of faith? If we have problems that bother us, we need to fix them now before we become a casualty. We must find the answers to matters that vex us, that leave dangerously gaping holes in our faith. We are in the battle right now. We're on enemy territory as it stands. We want our faith to be bulletproof.

The helmet of salvation is another essential piece of armor. Salvation comes in three forms: justification, sanctification, and glorification - past present and future. We were justified when we asked Christ's forgiveness, and every day we are continually being sanctified by the Holy Spirit. We all look forward to our future glorification, when we are living forever with our Savior. Head shots can kill us as quickly as chest shots, and salvation covers and protects our spiritual head, keeping us safe from efforts of the enemy to destroy our minds and understanding. When we hand ourselves over to Christ as a living sacrifice, He makes possible the renewing of our minds so that we can have the mind of Christ:

> *And be not conformed to this world: but*
> *be ye transformed by the renewing of your*
> *mind, that ye may prove what is that good,*
> *and acceptable, and perfect, will of God.*
>
> Romans 12:2

Just owning a helmet isn't any good. We have to have it strapped securely on our heads

We all know and love the Sword of the Spirit as the word of God. That's the only offensive weapon we have, by the way. All other items listed here in

Ephesians 6 - shield, helmet, belt - are defensive in nature. The sword is a two-edged sword, according to Hebrews:

> *For the word of God is quick, and powerful, and sharper than any two-edged sword, piercing even to the dividing asunder of soul and spirit, and of the joints and marrow, and is a discerner of the thoughts and intents of the heart.*

Hebrews 4:12

It is interesting that the technology of those early centuries seemed to favor a long, curved sword. Most armies were equipped with a long sword, but the Roman army did something rather different. They developed a short, double-edged sword only about 24-inches long. With that short sword, they conquered the world, but it was a close-in weapon. This meant the soldiers had to know how to use it and they had to practice, practice, practice with it. The same is true regarding the Word of God. Every time Satan came at Jesus with a temptation, Jesus hammered back with, "It is written!" If we don't know what the Bible says, we can't use it very well. It does little good sitting on our bookshelf; it must get stored in a readily available place in our minds and hearts. That means using it every day.

## The Heavy Artillery

We Christians often talk about these pieces of armor listed in Ephesians 6, but we often fail to recognize the most important verse: Verse 18.

*Praying always with all prayer and supplication in the Spirit, and watching thereunto with all perseverance and supplication for all saints;*

Ephesians 6:18

That right there is our greatest weapon. We have the Sword of the Spirit as an offensive weapon to parry Satan's blows and take down the enemy's stronghold of deception. However, our prayers are the heavy artillery in the heavenlies. When we pray, God works to destroy the plans of the enemy and to bring His power and love and light into any situation. When we can't find our children, we can ask our Lord, "Jesus, please send them home." We have the ability to come to the aid of our Christian brothers and sisters being persecuted in Iranian or North Korean prisons through our prayers and supplications. We can participate in helping those being assassinated in Egypt or Iraq or Burma without getting on an airplane. We can pray for our civil leaders, for our Supreme Court, for the governors in our states. Whether we like the person in office, whether we agree with his policies or not, we can pray that God's power and will are at work in the Oval

Office, to accomplish His purposes no matter what wickedness is intended by the prince of this world.

Our prayer closet is more powerful than the ballot box. I want you to notice what Paul prays for. He encourages us to pray always every day for the saints. We need to pray for each other. It is a warfare, and we cover each other's backs through prayer.

Paul tells the Ephesians to pray for all the saints, but he also seeks prayer for himself:

*And for me, that utterance may be given unto me, that I may open my mouth boldly, to make known the mystery of the gospel, For which I am an ambassador in bonds: that therein I may speak boldly, as I ought to speak.*

Ephesians 6:19-20

Imagine Paul asking for boldness. I'm always amused as I visualize him writing this letter, because I know he had a Praetorian Guard chained to him. Why was the guard chained there? So he couldn't get away. Can you imagine being chained to Paul for a full shift? We learn in Philippians 1:12-13 that the whole palace guard knew of his situation and had heard the Gospel. Yet, Paul the fiery apostle, Paul himself seeks the prayers of the Ephesians here at the end of Ephesians 6. He wants them to pray that he would be able to speak boldly according to what he needs to speak.

If Paul needed that prayer, we all need it. We all need to pray for one another all the time, seeking the guidance of the Holy Spirit as we do so.

## Seeing Him As He Is

This world is a war zone, but we know the Victor. In just a little while, it will all be over, and we will see Christ face to face.

> *Beloved, now are we the sons of God, and it doth not yet appear what we shall be: but we know that, when he shall appear, we shall be like him; for we shall see him as he is.*

1 John 3:2

We know that we are the children of God, but we have no capacity to understand what God is like. We are locked away in our four-dimensional world right now. If I took a photograph of you, I would end up with a two-dimensional representation of a three-dimensional being. A hologram, on the other hand, is a three-dimensional representation, and I could understand you best by being a three-dimensional being with you. One day we will be able to see God as He is, because we will be like Him.

How many dimensions does Christ have in His resurrected body? We know he has more than our four space-time dimensions.

Jesus walks to Emmaus with two disciples in Luke 24. When they reach their destination, they beg Him to stay, so He sits down to eat with them. After He blesses the food, He suddenly disappears in verse 31. Just a few verses later, we find the disciples hiding together. Jesus doesn't bother knocking at the door to enter the room. No, He just appears there before them. The room has three-dimensions - four walls, a ceiling and floor, and Jesus manages to show up without the nuisance of going through any outer walls of the room. The disciples are frightened because the doors are locked and the windows are shut and Jesus just appears. They think He's a ghost or a spirit, but He wants them to know He's a physical being:

*And as they thus spake, Jesus himself stood in the midst of them, and saith unto them, Peace be unto you. But they were terrified and affrighted, and supposed that they had seen a spirit. And he said unto them, Why are ye troubled? and why do thoughts arise in your hearts? Behold my hands and my feet, that it is I myself: handle me, and see; for a spirit hath not flesh and bones, as ye see me have. And when he had thus spoken, he shewed them his hands and his feet. And while they yet believed not for joy, and wondered, he said unto them, Have ye here any meat? And they gave him a piece of a broiled fish, and of an honeycomb. And he took it, and did eat before them.*

Luke 24:36-43

He asks them to give Him some food, and He eats it. He has them put their hands on Him, to see that He's really standing there. He demonstrates that He is a physical being, but He had become somebody no longer limited to three spatial dimensions.

One day we too will have glorified, resurrected bodies. One day, we will be able to live in more than these three limited dimensions of space. We will be able to see Him as He really is, because we will be like Him. We won't be equal to Him of course; He is the Creator and King of the universe. However, we will be able to comprehend Him in all His fullness, and that will be a wonderful, exciting day indeed.

When Adam turned his back on the commandment of God, he forfeited his earthly dominion to Satan. The last Adam, Christ, gained dominion over everything, including the angels.

*Wherefore God also hath highly exalted him, and given him a name which is above every name: That at the name of Jesus every knee should bow, of things in heaven, and things in earth, and things under the earth; And that every tongue should confess that Jesus Christ is Lord, to the glory of God the Father.*

Philippians 2:9-11

*Thou hast put all things in subjection under his feet. For in that he put all in subjection under him, he left nothing that is not put under him. But now we see not yet all things put under him.*

Hebrews 2:8

Things in heaven and things in earth and things under the earth - all will be in subjection under Him. For He must reign, till He hath put all enemies under His feet, and the last enemy that shall be destroyed is death. Eventually, you and I will find everlasting joy in joining hands with Him.

*What shall we then say to these things? If God be for us, who can be against us? He that spared not his own Son, but delivered him up for us all, how shall he not with him also freely give us all things? Who shall lay any thing to the charge of God's elect? It is God that justifieth. Who is he that condemneth? It is Christ that died, yea rather, that is risen again, who is even at the right hand of God, who also maketh intercession for us. Who shall separate us from the love of Christ? shall tribulation, or distress,*

*or persecution, or famine, or nakedness,*
*or peril, or sword? As it is written,*
*For thy sake we are killed all the day long;*
*we are accounted as sheep for the slaughter.*
*Nay, in all these things we are more than*
*conquerors through him that loved us.*
*For I am persuaded, that neither death,*
*nor life, nor angels, nor principalities, nor*
*powers, nor things present, nor things to*
*come, Nor height, nor depth, nor any other*
*creature, shall be able to separate us from*
*the love of God, which is in Christ Jesus*
*our Lord.*

Romans 8:31-39

I'm not a Republican nor a Democrat. I'm a Monarchist, and my candidate is King of the Jews. He's the King of all ages, the King of heaven, the King of glory, King of kings and Lord of lords. He's the miracle of all the ages.

You and I are the beneficiaries of a love letter. It was written in blood on a wooden cross erected in Judea 2000 years ago. He was crucified on a cross of wood, yet He made the hill on which it stood. What held Him to that cross? It wasn't the nails. At any time He could have said, "Enough already. I am outta here." What held Him to the cross? It was His love for you and me. He was born of a woman, so you and I can be born again. He humbled Himself so that we could be lifted up. He became a servant so that we could be joint heirs with him. He suffered rejection so that we could become His friends. He denied Himself so that we could freely receive all things. He gave Himself so that He could bless us in every way.

I look forward to seeing Him as He is. I look forward to that day in humble awe.

*Father, we thank You that we have such a King. We pray, Father, that You would illuminate what You would have of each of us in the days ahead, that we might be more responsive to Your will in our lives. We long to be effective stewards of the opportunities You bring before us. We ask all of these things, Father, that we might be more pleasing in Your sight. May we grow in grace and knowledge of Your Son as we commit ourselves without reservations into Your hands. In the name of Yeshua, our Lord, our Savior, our King, our Messiah indeed. Amen.*

# Endnotes

1   Matthew 6:9-13, esp. v.13

2   John 12:31, 14:30, 16:11

3   Ezekiel 28: 12-17

4   Revelation 2:7; 22:2

5   Genesis 3:24

6   Revelation 12:12 tells us that the Devil's wrath will be great toward the end because he knows his time is limited.

7   John 19:10-11

8   See our studies *Thy Kingdom Come* and *Behold the Fifth Horseman*.

9   Matthew 25:41

10  Job 42:16

11  Revelation 12:3-4

12  Psalm 37:35-36; 73:12-18

13  Bergquist, L. (1999). *Swedenborg's Secret* (142-155). London: The Swedenborg Society.

14  McKeegan, K et al. (2011). The Oxygen Isotopic Composition of the Sun Inferred from Captured Solar Wind. *Science*, 332(6037): 1528-1532.

15  Staff writers, (2011, June 24). NASA Mission Suggests Sun and Planets Constructed Differently. *Space Daily*. Retrieved on April 25, 2016 from SpaceDaily.com

16  Hanna, W. ed. (1857). "Selected works of Thomas Chalmers" *Natural Theology*. Volume 5 (p. 146). Edinburgh: Thomas Constable.

17  James 4:6; 1 Peter 5:5

18  Proverbs 16:18

19  Luke 10:17-18

20  Matthew 16:18

21  Our *Beyond Perception* study deals with these matters in more detail.

22  Aspect, A., Dalibard, J., & Roger, G. (1982). Experimental Test of Bell's Inequalities Using Time-Varying Analyzers. *Physical Review Letters*, 49, 1804-1807.

23  Matthew 12:43-45

24  Matthew 8:31

25  Of course, I'm joking about the bazookas – although I'm sure Ben Hadad would have used them if he'd had them.

26  Jude 1:9

27  1 Thessalonians 4:16

28  James 5:16

29  Psalm 2:9; Revelation 2:27, 19:15

30  Daniel 9:27; Revelation 11:2-3, 12:6, 13:5

31  Psalm 2:9, Revelation 2:27, 12:5, 19:15

32  Genesis 6:9

33  Genesis 15:13-16

34  Deuteronomy 20:10-18

35  Matthew 2:13-18

36  Luke 4:29-30

37  Mark 4:37-41

38  Romans 8:37

39  Psalm 91:12

# About the Author

**Chuck Missler**
*Founder, Koinonia House*

Chuck Missler was raised in Southern California.

Chuck demonstrated an aptitude for technical interests as a youth. He became a ham radio operator at age nine and started piloting airplanes as a teenager. While still in high school, Chuck built a digital computer in the family garage.

His plans to pursue a doctorate in electrical engineering at Stanford University were interrupted when he received a Congressional appointment to the United States Naval Academy at Annapolis. Graduating with honors, Chuck took his commission in the Air Force. After completing flight training, he met and married Nancy (who later founded The King's High Way ministry). Chuck joined the Missile Program and eventually became Branch Chief of the Department of Guided Missiles.

Chuck made the transition from the military to the private sector when he became a systems engineer with TRW, a large aerospace firm. He then went on to serve as a senior analyst with a non-profit think tank where he conducted projects for the intelligence community and the Department of Defense. During that time, Chuck earned a master's degree in engineering at UCLA, supplementing previous graduate work in applied mathematics, advanced statistics and information sciences.

Recruited into senior management at the Ford Motor Company in Dearborn, Michigan, Chuck established the first international computer network in 1966. He left Ford to start his own company, a computer network firm that was subsequently acquired by Automatic Data Processing (listed on the New York Stock Exchange) to become its Network Services Division.

As Chuck notes, his day of reckoning came in the early '90s when — as the result of a merger — he found himself the chairman and a major shareholder of a small, publicly owned development company known as Phoenix Group International. The firm established an $8 billion joint venture with the Soviet Union to supply personal computers to their 143,000 schools. Due to several unforeseen circumstances, the venture failed. The Misslers lost everything, including their home, automobiles and insurance.

It was during this difficult time that Chuck turned to God and the Bible. As a child he developed an intense interest in the Bible; studying it became a favorite pastime. In the 1970s, while still in the corporate world, Chuck began leading weekly Bible studies at the 30,000 member Calvary Chapel Costa Mesa, in California. He and Nancy established Koinonia House in 1973, an organization devoted to encouraging people to study the Bible.

Chuck had enjoyed a longtime, personal relationship with Hal Lindsey, who upon hearing of Chuck's professional misfortune, convinced him that he could easily succeed as an independent author and speaker. Over the years, Chuck had developed a loyal following. (Through Doug Wetmore, head of the tape ministry of Firefighters for Christ, Chuck learned that over 7 million copies of his taped Bible studies were scattered throughout the world.) Koinonia House then became Chuck's full-time profession.

Chuck Missler moved with his late wife, Nancy, from the United States to New Zealand in 2010, after many previous visits there. Chuck established a new South Pacific base for Koinonia House, and a new home for himself and Nancy in Reporoa, a small town located in the Waikato region of the country. Chuck originated all his new materials from the new headquarters at the River Lodge before his retirement in 2016.

Chuck passed away in May, 2018.